SOUL-SOOTHING STORIES of
Cancer Survivors

An inspirational tribute to the BRAVERY of SURVIVORSHIP

More than *50* stories of cancer survivors

by Heidi Leist

Photos by Bryan Leist

This book is intended as a reference volume only, not as a medical manual. The information given here is designed to inspire and inform. It is not intended as a substitute for any treatment that may have been prescribed by your doctor. If you suspect that you have a medical problem, we urge you to seek competent medical help.

Internet addresses given in this book were accurate at the time it went to press.

© 2017 by Lemongrass Spa Products

All rights reserved. No part of this publication may be reproduced or transmitted in any form or by any means, electronic or mechanical, including photocopying, recording, or any other information storage and retrieval system, without the written permission of the publisher.

The mark Lemongrass Spa® is a registered trademark of Lemongrass Spa Products. Any use of this mark without the permission of the publisher is unauthorized. This publication also includes references to third party trademarks, which are owned and may be registered by third parties whose products are reviewed in this publication. Any and all unauthorized uses of these third party marks are also prohibited.

Printed in the United States of America

Cover design by Leanne Coppola

Book design by Susan Eugster

Photography by Bryan Leist

Photo page 190 courtesy of Gary Pack Photography

Library of Congress Control Number 2017915643
ISBN 978-1-950459-17-9

2 4 6 8 10 9 7 5 3 paperback

To my husband, Bryan, and our beautiful daughters, Emily and Clara, who inspire me every day to be the best wife and mother I can be.

To my mom, Karen, who inspires me to be kind, compassionate, hardworking, and faithful. To my dad, Millard, who encouraged an entrepreneurial mindset and taught me the art of sales. To Kim, John, and my extended family for their compassion and positive encouragement. To Jim and Robin for their helpfulness, advice, and honest feedback.

To anyone who's been diagnosed with cancer and for the bravery their families have shown during their journeys.

To my tribe of leaders, who continually inspire me to make our organization the best direct sales company in the country.

To my entire corporate team at Lemongrass Spa Products, who create life-changing products. To Heather Johnson and Angie Conrad for compiling stories for this exceptional project.

To the talented Jennifer Bright Reich and Jennifer Schriffert for their vision of the Soul Soothing Stories concept. To the dedicated team at Momosa Publishing for their editing and research every step of the way.

To God for His abundant blessings and for very specifically giving me an opportunity to pour into the lives of others in a way that brings glory to Him.

Contents

A TRIBUTE TO STELLA   VII
INTRODUCTION   XI

Part 1:
The Importance of Early Detection   1

Screening Saved Her Life   5
Following His Mom's Advice   9
Heeding Her Intuition   13
Surviving the Whirlwind   17
Listening to Her Gut   21
Making—or *Taking*—the Time   25
Believing that Things Will Be Okay   29
Enjoying Her Life—Again   35

Part 2:
Finding Your Village   39

Navigating a Bump in His Road   43
Accepting Help—and Love—From Family and Friends   45
Traversing Her Meandering Path   49
Circling Her Wagons of Friends   53
Finding Support in a City Rich with Help   57
Growing Her Community of Support   61

Part 3:
Keeping the Faith in God—and Medicine   67

Attracting Positivity and Hope   71
Finding Strength in Her "Prayer Closet"   75
Keeping the Faith and Confidence   79
Working Through Her List   83
Drawing on Her Faith   87
Living Her Life Guided by Her Faith   91
Finding Unexpected Strength   95
Feeling Grateful Despite Her Challenges   99
Summoning the Angels—and a Vacuum Cleaner   103
Praying for a Cure   109
Trusting in God's Plan   115

Part 4:
Choosing a Natural, Chemical-Free Life 123

Healing with Natural Products 127
Changing—for the Better 131
Arming Herself with Information 135
Choosing Safer Skin Care Products 139
Helping Others Choose Healthier Products 143
Taking a Natural Approach 147

Part 5:
Staying Brave—Despite Adversity 153

Taking Time to Re-Focus 157
Wearing Her Baldness Proudly 161
Courageously Choosing to *Live* 165
Bravely Accepting Help 169
Returning to Her Glorious Mediocrity 173
Focusing on What She *Could* Keep 177
Fighting to Survive 181
Savoring the Sweet 185

Part 6:
Finding a Way to Give Back 191

Dressing Up for Chemo 195
Marching to Help Others 199
Helping Her Bosom Buddies 203
Going from Customer to Consultant 207
Gifting for Good 211
Thriving—not Just Surviving 215
Creating a *New* Good Place 219
Making Connections 223
Providing Pick-Me-Ups 229
Fighting Back with Style and Grace 231

ABOUT THE AUTHOR AND PHOTOGRAPHER 235
ABOUT LEMONGRASS SPA 237
AFTERWORD: MAKING LIFESTYLE CHANGES 239

Wayne and Stella McEwen, 1941

Stella at her lake home after she retired.

A Tribute to Stella

A heart of gold that held more love than you can imagine—that was our mom, Stella. She was our ray of sunshine!

Stella McEwen was a wife and mother of five—me, my three sisters, and my brother, ages 10 to 21—when she received the breast cancer diagnosis in 1965. She had found a small lump under her armpit while showering. Her doctor, the only surgeon in the small Minnesota town, scheduled her to have a radical mastectomy with lymph gland removal in her right breast. Dad went to research this cancer at the library and learned statistically there was a very low survival rate, but also found hope in reading that there was a good chance of complete recovery if there was no reocurring cancer within five years.

The day of the surgery came. I remember Dad was devastated as he sat out in the waiting room.

"She doesn't have much of a chance," he said to me. This quiet man had survived Navy battles on a destroyer ship during WWII for four years with his wife waiting for his return. Now he was facing their toughest battle with his sweetheart on the operating table.

> *"Some people come into our lives, leave prints on our hearts, and we are never the same."*

Life was joyful in their relationship up to this moment. With the cancer fear, now the mission was "saving Mom." She endured numerous doctors' visits and a trip to the Mayo Clinic after the surgery and radiation treatments to stave off any remaining cells. Her three young daughters kept her upbeat and busy with school events and summer activities at the countryside lake home where they lived.

A few years after the diagnosis of the cancer, her first granddaughter, Heidi, was born, just one day before her own birthday. Then a grandson was born a few months later, and her focus shifted to being a grandmother! Knitting and crocheting became therapy for her swollen arm from the edema due to the lymph gland removal and painful days with antibiotics. She knitted afghans and blankets for each family member—for every new baby born and one for all the graduates in the family too!

Stella made us laugh and feel loved again. She counted her blessings and was strong and capable, and the joyful laughter returned, with her husband and growing family embracing her.

Stella was a survivor, living 37 more years after cancer until the age of 83. Her love of life and family was contagious and inspiring. There was always kindness from Stella; a glowing smile, a cute giggle, and a loving embrace.

—*By Karen Voeltz, Heidi Voeltz Leist's mom*

A Tribute to Stella

Stella enjoyed hosting picnics at her lakeside home with her five children and grandchildren. From left: Patti, Lila, Cheryl, Lynn, Karen and Stella.

Stella loved entertaining her 13 grandchildren at her home in Minnesota. Joshua, Bobby, Heather, Andy, Cory, Nathan, Wade, Laura, Mike, Carrie, John, Kim, and Heidi.

Introduction

For years, I received personal testimonials from customers who used our natural skincare products. They raved about how much better their skin looked and felt after applying our crèmes, balms, and body butters. Even people with the worst skin conditions commented on how much of an improvement they saw with just an application or two.

Our Lemongrass Spa Consultants started giving these products as gifts to cancer patients, and nurses began recommending them to people going through chemotherapy and radiation because they saw first-hand just how effective our handcrafted moisturizers worked to repair skin's natural oils.

We began receiving stories and feedback from many brave people battling cancer. The most heartbreaking were the stories from parents of young children. We read how difficult it was for children to undergo the nausea, fatigue, and anxiety associated with treatment, and also how much damage it did to their delicate skin. We saw pictures of tiny hands that were practically unrecognizable as a result of the extreme dryness and irritation.

When stories like these came in from customers, our consultants and our home office would send them a complimentary trial jar of Ultra Hydrating Body Crème or Organic Nail Balm with a note of encouragement. Many found relief and would order more.

Word spread quickly as consultants shared these powerful testimonials at their spa parties and on social media. One day, I received an email from a clever consultant with the suggestion that we package three items together to be able to give to patients. So, in 2013 we began offering our Cancer Care Set, which was eventually renamed the Loving Care Gift Set. The Organic Nail Balm in a Tube, Healing Elements Balm, and Ultra Hydrating Body Crème became the magical trio, lovingly packaged in a pink or gray organza bag. Hundreds of them were ordered that year, and story after story flooded our inboxes.

In honor of Breast Cancer Awareness Month in October 2014, I decided that our corporate office would expand this program. We decided to offer Loving Care Gift Sets, free of charge, to anyone diagnosed with any type of cancer. The only prerequisite was that the recipient be nominated for the gift set by a loved one. Eloquently written nomination letters poured in, and patients with tear-filled eyes gratefully accepted the gifts that arrived on their doorsteps. Each package included a card to let them know that someone special had requested it on their behalf.

We continued the initiative each year, and the numbers multiplied. Hundreds of our customers took the time to nominate that special someone. Whether it was for a mother diagnosed with breast cancer, a daughter with melanoma, a father with prostate cancer, a son with lymphoma, or a husband with a brain tumor, these complimentary gifts helped hundreds of deserving people. Our Facebook feed was filled with these heartfelt stories of gratitude, and our home office team rejoiced in the success of the program.

"We are truly a company with a heart," our sales leaders remarked.

When you've walked the journey alongside someone with cancer, there's a sense of helplessness. It's often difficult to find the right words of encouragement when you see how much pain and discouragement they endure. Having something to give a loved one that spoke for itself seemed to appeal to all of us.

When the news came that my 43-year-old sister-in-law had breast cancer, the entire family was in shock. She was an athletic mom of three, health conscious, well educated, and careful about what she purchased for herself and her family. Many times, words didn't come easy, but sending a loving care gift set or a bottle of bath crystals was something she treasured. The herbal foot kit was one of her favorite ways to relax with her girlfriends and feel comforted by her family as she went through extensive chemotherapy and radiation.

When my friend Heather found out her husband, Jeff, had a very rare brain tumor, she made sure she had Healing Elements Balm and Whipped Body Butter for him after his laser surgery. As a fire fighter, he had used these ointments on scars he'd received when hot embers touched his exposed skin during harrowing wildfires in Colorado.

As a breast cancer survivor, my grandmother Stella was an inspiration to me as a young child. I saw how she had bravely endured a radical mastectomy in her forties, and because of that had one arm that was much larger than her unscathed one. She took everything in stride with a smile on her face and a giggle that was contagious. It was because of her that I was passionate about creating products that were safe, healthy, and oh, so amazing for skin.

The stories lovingly shared in this book are intended to be a source of light and hope for you or someone you care about. It fills our hearts when we can passionately bring resilience, joy, renewed faith, and comfort to those around us.

Introduction

Part 1

THE IMPORTANCE OF
EARLY DETECTION

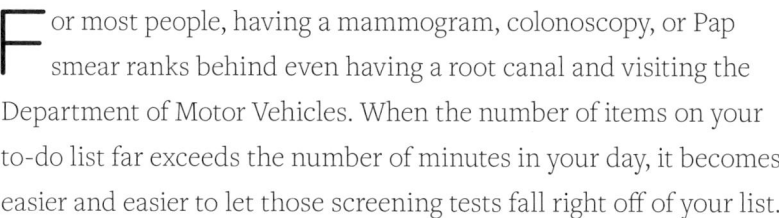

For most people, having a mammogram, colonoscopy, or Pap smear ranks behind even having a root canal and visiting the Department of Motor Vehicles. When the number of items on your to-do list far exceeds the number of minutes in your day, it becomes easier and easier to let those screening tests fall right off of your list.

But what if bumping that screening up on your to-do list could actually add years to your life and life to your years?

Bet you'd make time for it!

According to the National Cancer Institute, patients whose cancers are detected and treated early may have better long term survival than people whose cancer was found—and treated—later, after symptoms appear.

Screening simply saves lives. Once annual Pap tests became common in the United States, deaths from cervical cancer declined sharply. Screenings for both breast cancer and colorectal cancer have also decreased deaths from those cancers.

Screening tests, like colonoscopies, mammograms, medical thermography, Pap tests, and prostate specific antigen tests, find cancer before it starts to cause signs and symptoms. They can find cancer early—when the chances of surviving—and thriving—are highest.

It's important to remember that the person who knows most about your body is you. Pay attention to your body; listen to its clues about your health. A change could be your body's way of trying to get

"People should be afraid of the cancer, not the mammogram."

—NANCY REAGAN

your attention. Listen to your body when it whispers, before it needs to yell. A change in weight, birthmarks or moles, bowel habits, sleep habits—any of these things are a reason to schedule a chat with your doctor. And certainly, honor your body with a monthly breast or testicular self-exam.

Scientists and researchers are racing the clock, developing new technologies and pursuing key opportunities, trying to develop new ways to detect cancer. For example, experts are developing technologies called "liquid biopsies" that can noninvasively identify the presence of genetic material from cancer cells in the blood or molecular markers in urine or saliva that can identify precursor lesions or cancer at its earliest stages.

Other scientists are identifying genetic changes that point to potential avenues for more effectively monitoring people at increased risk of cancer.

Some cancers are dramatically more treatable when caught early. Colorectal cancer, for example, is 90 percent beatable—if it's caught early.

Make the time—take the time—to save yourself your precious time.

Screening Saved Her Life

Two years ago, 65-year-old Carol Urbaniak, of Argyle, Minnesota, had a routine mammogram, which found a spot under her breast. It was so small that her doctor wasn't concerned and didn't order a biopsy.

"I never even thought it was cancer," Carol said.

A year later, the mass had grown. This time, Carol underwent a biopsy. At the time of the test, she was told that she had a moderate chance of having cancer. The doctor who performed the biopsy told Carol, "I want to be up front with you, so if it is cancer, it won't shock you."

That was a Friday, and Carol had to wait four days—until the following Tuesday—before she got the call with the results.

"After that biopsy, that was probably the most anxious time for me," Carol said.

Carol works as a caregiver in a group home. One day, while she was driving a patient to a doctor's appointment, she found herself wondering, *How do people handle not knowing?*

The call came, and the news wasn't good. The tumor was malignant.

"When I did find out, even though it was cancer, at least I could move forward and deal with it," Carol said.

Carol ended up having a mastectomy. Because the cancer hadn't spread, she didn't need chemotherapy or radiation treatment. However, in a follow-up appointment, her doctor found cancer in additional tissue that needed to be removed, so she needed a second surgery.

Fortunately, both the surgeries and Carol's recovery went well.

"I feel like I was so blessed compared to what other people have gone through," Carol said.

Carol and her family didn't dwell on the fact that she had cancer. Instead, they focused on the surgeries. Although Carol was surprised by how emotional she felt, she told herself, *This is happening, and we're going to deal with it.*

Her husband, two adult sons, who are 44 and 29, their wives, and her grandchildren, who range in age from seven months to 22 years old, helped her through it, along with her friends, who visited, called, and texted to make sure she was doing okay.

Carol's doctor recommended physical therapy so Carol diligently went to physical therapy, doing her exercises at home as well. She also relied on prayer and attending church for the support she needed to help her through. Members of her church family even brought her meals for a couple of weeks.

"I could definitely feel the prayers," Carol said, and she prayed for strength and understanding.

Today, Carol takes hormone therapy. To her disappointment, the hot flashes she experienced during menopause are back.

"I had forgotten about them, and now I'm back at it again," Carol

> *"Cancer is a word, not a sentence."*
> —JOHN DIAMON

said, but she can see the bright side. "They're uncomfortable, but Minnesota winters are cold," she said. Thankfully, the hot flashes don't interrupt her sleep.

Carol chose not to have reconstructive breast surgery. While considering it, she met with one woman who had a double mastectomy and had reconstructive surgery and another woman who had a single mastectomy and chose not to. She also met with a plastic surgeon to get information on the surgery. In the end, she didn't feel that the reconstruction was necessary. Today she's satisfied with her decision.

As a result of Carol's experience with breast cancer, she's an advocate for screening and early detection.

"I can't stress enough the importance of having yearly mammograms," Carol said.

Mammograms lower the risk of dying from breast cancer by 14 percent for women ages 50 to 59 and by 33 percent for women ages 60 to 69, according to the nonprofit Susan G. Komen organization, which used data from the 2016 U.S. Preventive Services Task Force.

"I'm absolutely so thankful that we found it in time," Carol said.

Following His Mom's Advice

Jerry Michalski, 37, a fruit expert at Edible Arrangements in Philadelphia, Pennsylvania, began following the advice of his mother, a nurse, after he got out of college: He gave himself monthly testicular self-exams. It became a lifesaving habit.

Physicians aren't the ones who find most cases of testicular cancer, which is the most common cancer among men ages 15 to 35. Most testicular cancers are found by men themselves or by their partners, according to the Testicular Cancer Society. When testicular cancer is caught early, men have a nearly 100 percent survival rate.

For Jerry, it all began with a case of the flu in February 2016. After the illness ran its course, Jerry expected to feel back to normal again, but he didn't. He had fatigue and pain that was shooting down his legs. An orthopedic specialist ordered an X-ray and told him he had arthritis.

But the pain and fatigue continued.

"I didn't want to get out of bed," Jerry said. "My eating habits were all over the place. I felt really run down."

> *"Every day that I challenge this cancer and survive is a victory for me."*
>
> —INGRID BERGMAN

Jerry was used to walking four to six miles a day in the city, but his energy was so sapped that he could walk only about one mile.

One night, as was Jerry's habit, he did a testicular self-exam. He had pain and swelling, but he thought he must have accidentally hit his testicle on something.

"I asked my girlfriend, Laura, to look at it, and I said, 'Ouch,'" Jerry said.

Jerry didn't delay seeing his primary doctor, who did an ultrasound and referred him to a urologist. Within 48 hours of the results coming back, Jerry was told that he had testicular cancer and needed immediate surgery. The surgeon removed a tumor that was two centimeters long and one centimeter wide.

Recovery from surgery was hard. It was painful for Jerry to sit up, and he could barely walk up and down the stairs. But he got through it.

Unfortunately, Jerry's cancer scare wasn't over. During Jerry's follow-up with the doctor, an ultrasound picked up additional tumors in the other testicle. He needed another surgery to have them removed. The second surgery was followed by chemotherapy a few months later.

One of the hardest things for Jerry to come to terms with is the knowledge that he can't have kids of his own.

"It hurts to this day, and it probably will hurt forever," Jerry said. "It will hurt for the rest of my life."

But there has also been joy. Jerry married Laura in the fall.

The Importance of Early Detection

"She has been such a big help and has offered tremendous support through the whole thing," he said. "She holds me when I'm down. She talks sense into me when I'm not thinking straight. She's everything to me."

And going through cancer changed Jerry's view on life.

"Before, I was more concerned about myself," he said. "Today, I cherish every day because you don't know what's going to happen next."

Jerry is going to therapy. Through talking with his counselor, he has realized that in the past, he had trouble dealing with things emotionally.

"I physically kept going and didn't listen to my body," Jerry said. Now he's working on putting a different spin on things.

One thing is certain: Doing monthly self-exams saved Jerry's life. He was told that if he had waited another three months before seeing a doctor, the cancer might have moved into his bloodstream and could have been deadly. Now Jerry knows that slowing down, paying attention to what's happening in his body, and making emotional connections are the new habits that will help him to stay healthy.

Heeding Her Intuition

In 2016, cancer threw Sheila Alkire, 54, two punches—back to back.

In July of that year, Sheila, a training director in Germantown, Maryland, had a routine mammogram. It showed a small mass on her breast that required a partial mastectomy, which is now the preferred term for lumpectomy, which cured her breast cancer.

At the same time, Sheila was having trouble breathing. She was athletic, working out four to five days a week doing boot camp, strength training, or running. But suddenly, Sheila found herself struggling to breathe after going up two sets of stairs.

For several months, Sheila saw doctors, who diagnosed her with upper respiratory infections, sinus infections, and bronchitis. However, the treatments for these conditions never took care of the problem.

"Believe it or not, I was still going to boot camp and running," Sheila said. "But I had to stop more frequently to catch my breath, and I had to walk instead of run up hills."

The problem only got worse. When Sheila ate, she started to feel like she was choking. And despite feeling tired, she couldn't lie down to sleep. She had to sleep sitting up because it was hard to breathe. One day, Sheila was even struggling to breathe while talking to her mom on the phone.

"We're going to the emergency room right now," Sheila's mom said.

There, doctors took a chest X-ray. They found a seven-centimeter mass on Sheila's chest. She later learned that she had squamous cell lung cancer. The tumor was sitting on top of her trachea (windpipe). Sheila spent 17 days in the hospital. Five of those days were in the intensive care unit until doctors could perform a biopsy. That was followed by intensive radiation therapy in the hospital to shrink the tumor quickly and allow Sheila to breathe more easily.

When Sheila could finally breathe well again, she went home. But after that, she needed more aggressive radiation and chemotherapy.

"The treatments really knocked me down," Sheila said. "I was extremely tired. I was sick."

Because of all of the treatments, Sheila became violently ill and dehydrated. She had to spend another two stays in the hospital to treat her dehydration. She lost 15 pounds and felt weak.

Throughout her treatment, Sheila worked full-time.

"Working helped to take my mind off of being sick," Sheila said. "Work forced me to get out of bed when all I really wanted to do was to watch TV with my two cats."

Sheila is grateful that she has a good employer, and she didn't have to worry about losing her job during her treatment.

Meanwhile, Sheila's mother and close friends helped her through every step of her journey. They made her soup, stayed with her, and drove her to appointments when she couldn't drive herself. When

> ## *"Energy and persistence conquer all things."*
>
> —BENJAMIN FRANKLIN

Sheila's hair began falling out, her hairdresser came to her house to cut it, eventually shaved her head, helped her pick out wigs, and then trimmed her wigs for her.

As time went on, Sheila ticked more and more treatments off her list, her energy started coming back, and she felt better.

In November, Sheila finished radiation. She completed her six rounds of chemotherapy in 2017. Today, Sheila is cancer-free, and she feels great.

"I have energy!" Sheila said. "I'm happy that I'm back in the gym. It's frustrating that I'm not as fast and quick as I was five months ago, but I know that my energy level will come back."

Sheila's dramatic recovery was helped because she was strong physically and mentally, but she realized that one lesson she learned from cancer is to slow down a bit.

"I tend to go mach 10 and be anal retentive about things," Sheila said. "I used to think, *It has to be done right away*. Now I ask, *Does it really need to be?*"

Sheila's experience gave her a greater appreciation for life. She has decided to go to London and to travel more often.

"I'm going to do the things that I've held back on," Sheila said. That includes volunteering and working with cancer patients.

In retrospect, Sheila wishes that she had insisted on getting an X-ray earlier, back when she was being told the cause of her breathing problems was bronchitis or another infection. Fortunately, Sheila's doctors caught her cancer early enough that it hadn't spread. She was told the type of lung cancer she had can move to the brain and stomach quickly. Because Sheila listened to her body and kept looking for answers, that didn't happen to her.

"Never ignore the feeling that something isn't right," Sheila said.

Surviving the Whirlwind

As 2016 began, life was good for Fargo, North Dakota, resident Amy Jacobson.

The proud mom of a 12-year-old daughter and a 20-year-old son, Amy had a great relationship with Kenny, her partner of 26 years. While Amy knew that she "wasn't 21 any longer," she still energetically embraced her life. The 46-year-old insurance company project manager was busy with her daughter's soccer games, work, and church. She loved spending time with her family and friends.

There were no black clouds on the horizon.

Until there were.

Some years earlier, Amy's mom had been diagnosed with breast cancer at a relatively young age. Fortunately, Amy's mom had been the only person in the immediate family to battle the disease. While Amy and her sisters—one younger, one older—knew that it was a good idea to be vigilant about cancer prevention and screenings, Amy said that she didn't really give her health much thought.

Before Amy had reached age 40, she had her first mammogram.

Since that time, Amy had returned for mammograms at regular intervals—with no cause for concern or alarm. But right after New Year's Day in 2016, Amy noticed that something didn't feel quite right in one of her breasts.

"I could feel a mass when I was standing up, but not when I was lying or sitting down," Amy said.

At the end of the month, Amy went to see her primary care physician, who ordered a mammogram the same day. The next week, Amy had a stereotactic biopsy. That's a procedure that uses a computer and imaging performed in at least two areas to localize a suspect area in 3D and then guide the removal of tissue for examination by a pathologist under a microscope.

Amy isn't a fan of the procedure, calling it "awful," but she admits it was effective in diagnosing the mass.

"My doctor could see the mass right away," Amy said. "He was pretty certain even just from the image that it was cancer."

On February 9, the diagnosis was official.

After that, Amy and Kenny sought a second opinion to reconfirm the diagnosis.

That made it doubly official.

On March 15, Amy began 16 rounds of an AC-Taxol regimen, which is a chemotherapy combination that's used to treat breast cancer. She had her treatments at the nearby Sanford Medical Center in Fargo. About six weeks after the chemo sessions were over, Amy had a full mastectomy and reconstructive surgery. Following the surgery and reconstruction, Amy commenced a course of 33 radiation sessions, which finally ended in late November 2016.

Like many people undergoing chemo and radiation, Amy found that the intensive treatments were very hard on her skin. The chemo

> *"You never know how strong you are until being strong is the only choice you have."*
>
> —CAYLA MILLS

and radiation made Amy's skin more sensitive than it usually was.

"I was so grateful that I was introduced to Lemongrass Spa when the company was giving away free products to cancer patients," Amy said. "The products have tremendous healing properties for sensitive skin."

Today, Amy is thrilled to "feel like her old self again," but she admits that she had felt somewhat adrift at the end of the intensive treatment period.

"For months, when you're going through chemo, surgery, and radiation, the specialists tell you what to do, and you simply do it," Amy said. "I felt like I was operating on auto pilot."

Once the cancer no longer posed an immediate concern, Amy began a new life of regular appointments with her oncologist and radiologist. She admits that she always feels trepidation heading into them. But reflecting her Midwestern upbringing, Amy is stoic about the whole experience.

"I accepted that things like this happen," Amy said. "But I worried about my kids. I wondered, *Would I be there to see them become adults?* The thought that I might not be made me sad."

Amy's children had different ways of dealing with their mom's situation.

"My daughter is like me—quieter and not a worrier. She believed that everything would be fine," Amy said. "My diagnosis wasn't easy for my son, though. After the surgery, he asked, 'It's gone now, right?' I know he had a very hard time with everything."

Along with leaning on her faith and others close to her, Amy credits Kenny for being supportive.

"It was hard for Kenny as well," Amy said. "I know that he often thought, *I can drive her around to her appointments and treatments, but I can't have them for her.*"

Looking back now, Amy acknowledges the whirlwind that she has come through.

"It really was a rollercoaster," she said. "With the appointments, treatments, and procedures being so scheduled and regimented, there's very little time to actually *think* about what's happening and to process it all."

That's why Amy found the help and support of a psychosocial medical professional at Sanford to be so important.

"There was so much going on at once," Amy said. "For example, at first, I thought that I could handle losing my hair, but when it happened, it was so hard. And then my eyebrows and eyelashes fell out. That was difficult too. Taking steroids made me bloated as well. With all of those physical changes, I just didn't feel good about myself. I wasn't happy. The counselor gave me permission to feel what I needed to feel."

Today, Amy is grateful that she has put the whirlwind of cancer and its treatments in her past.

"Finally, I feel human again," Amy said. "You *do* come through it. You *do* get to the other side. In some ways, having cancer is sort of like having a baby. It changes your entire life."

Listening to Her Gut

"According to my medical team at Moffitt Cancer Center, I should be a 70-year-old overweight white male," said Kimberly Yang Elmhorst, 48, a community advocate in Lakeland, Florida, who has kids. "Well, I am not! I'm a 48-year-old Asian female who eats fairly sensibly, plays tennis, and works out several times a week."

In 2016, Kim went to the doctor because of stomach cramps, a low-grade fever, and blood in her stool. She has had light menstrual periods ever since undergoing endometrial ablation—a procedure that removes a thin layer of the uterine lining to treat very heavy bleeding—so the appearance of blood was worrying.

Kim's doctor doubted anything was wrong. But he ordered a colonoscopy for her peace of mind.

Because Kim was younger than 50, the test wasn't covered by insurance. Fortunately, she chose to pay the $1,800 bill out of pocket.

That decision most likely saved Kim's life.

When Kim woke up from the colonoscopy, her doctor said he found a large tumor at the beginning of her colon. It was so large that the doctor couldn't remove it and could not complete the colonoscopy, and she needed to see a surgeon immediately.

"I asked the dreaded question, 'Is it cancer?'" Kim said. "My doctor didn't say it was. But he also didn't say it wasn't."

Kim met with the surgeon the next day, who said he was treating the tumor like cancer until the pathology reports were back and that the tumor and part of her colon would have to be removed. A few days later, she learned it *was* colon cancer.

Surgery was scheduled for the following week.

"I kept asking myself, *How could my life change so drastically in 10 days*?" she said.

Kim's friends rallied around her and her family, offering prayers, meals, flowers, cards, and help with the kids.

"You name it, we were taken care of," Kim said.

But there was more bad news to come. After surgery, Kim's doctor told her the cancer had traveled and was found in lymph nodes that he had removed.

Kim felt devastated. "Are you kidding? We thought for sure the tumor would be removed and I would be all done," she said. "I thought to myself *I can't die. I have a great life with an amazing husband and wonderful children.*"

Kim left the hospital six days later prepared to begin 12 rounds of chemotherapy every other week at the beginning of August.

But first: heli-hiking.

Kim and her husband had planned a heli-hiking trip—in which hikers can explore remote mountain areas they can't access without a helicopter lift—in the Canadian Rocky Mountains for his 50th birthday. Her doctor didn't discourage the trip, so they rebooked their flight and went before her treatment began.

"Our 10-day trip was both frightening and invigorating," Kim said.

> *"God has a purpose for your pain, a reason for your struggles, and a reward for your faithfulness. Don't give up!"*

"It gave me the confidence to know I could conquer this mountain, too."

Then it was on to chemotherapy. Kim took two chemotherapy drugs. One of them had to be administered at the cancer center, and the other was administered to her through a pump at home. Kim was lucky that a friend of hers, who was an oncology nurse, could come to her house to detach the pump so she could avoid the 45-minute-drive to the cancer center for that treatment.

Soon after Kim's chemo began, the side effects began too. One of her first symptoms was a numb tongue, followed by numbness and tingling in her hands and feet. She lost her appetite and felt fatigued during the first few rounds, but she didn't experience nausea.

Another problem for Kim was that her white blood cell counts fell throughout her entire treatment. She needed a shot in between rounds of treatment to elevate her counts. Unfortunately, after the ninth round of treatments, Kim's counts stopped rebounding, and she fell behind on her treatments, which meant she was on chemotherapy longer than originally planned.

Kim worked hard to remain active throughout the treatments. When she felt well enough, she played tennis, walked three or more miles, and worked out with her trainer.

"Being active is a way of life for me, so during this time it was extremely important for me to keep this up as much as I could for my physical and mental well being," Kim said.

But she had to put her community work aside for eight months because she needed to avoid crowds and germs. She also wanted to focus her energy on treatment and exercise. It's something she was gradually able to pick up once treatment ended. She sits on several boards, is the current chair of Lakeland Vision, a community-driven program to make her town of Lakeland a better place to live, and raised a little more than $9 million when she chaired a United Way campaign.

Kim's support network helped along the way. Her husband brought her breakfast almost every morning of the seven months she was on chemo and "played Mom and Dad" when she was too sick to care for their children, 17 and 12, never once complaining.

"My husband definitely has the 'in sickness and in health' part down," she said. In the meantime, friends and family continued to bring her family meals, run errands for her, help with kids' activities, text, call, pray, and visit.

"We were overwhelmed with the love and support and never felt alone," Kim said. "You know people like you, but when something like this happens, you are overwhelmed by it."

Another guiding light for Kim was her faith.

"Early in my treatment, Kurt and I talked many times about how people get through something like this without faith in God," she said. "Through this chapter and for the next five years as I get checked and rechecked, I know that God has a plan."

In the meantime, Kim said she plans to live life to the fullest and enjoy every little blessing. One positive she can thank *herself* for: getting that colonoscopy when she thought something was wrong. Early detection means she's now cancer-free.

*Making—or **Taking**—the Time*

Taking the time to have an annual mammogram is difficult for most women. We all live busy lives, balancing work and family. To make matters worse, mammograms aren't the most comfortable experiences. It's hard to resign ourselves to doing something we know might be unpleasant—even painful. But the benefits to having an annual mammo far outweigh the discomfort.

Another impediment to scheduling an annual mammogram is the fear of finding out the news that you may have breast cancer. Avoiding the possibility of receiving that news is enough to keep some women putting off their mammograms to the next month.

Kita Heslinge, 71, a retired caregiver, was always religious about getting her mammograms done every year. Despite Kita's fears and the inconvenience of having a mammogram, she *made* time in her schedule to go.

Years went by with Kita faithfully having her mammograms—with no problems at all. Until Kita reached age 70.

Like every other year, in 2016, Kita went for her annual mammogram.

> *"You gain strength, courage, and confidence by every experience in which you really stop to look fear in the face. You must do the thing which you think you cannot do."*
>
> —ELEANOR ROOSEVELT

That year would prove to be quite different, however. The day after that mammogram, Kita received a call from her doctor asking her to come back in for some more tests.

Kita dutifully complied. She brought a book along with her to help pass the time in the waiting room. It never crossed Kita's mind to also bring along a supportive family member or friend.

"I assumed that they just saw a shadow on the film and that they needed to take another picture," Kita said.

Because Kita was so confident all was well, when she was finally brought back to meet with the doctor, and he explained the strong possibility that she could be facing breast cancer, Kita was shocked. The doctor explained that they would need to do another mammogram and a biopsy right away. He explained he suspected that she had a type of breast cancer called invasive ductal carcinoma.

This type of breast cancer is common. As its name implies, it's extremely invasive. This means the tumor is no longer localized in one area of the breast. Rather, it has spread into other parts of the breast tissue.

Because of this diagnosis, Kita's doctors told her that she would need a partial mastectomy and radiation treatments.

Thankfully, following the surgery Kita's doctor said that the cancer had not spread to her lymph nodes. Kita also had a DNA test to see if there was a risk for cancer anywhere else in her body. This test showed that Kita's body was not at risk for other cancers. These two factors kept her from having chemotherapy.

Over the next several months of treatment, Kita would face many challenges. In 2004, she had received a mechanical heart valve and had to be put on blood thinning medication for the rest of her life. In June of 2016, when she had the partial mastectomy, it caused clotting problems and she developed a large collection of blood at the surgical site. It took more than 90 days for the hematoma to resolve, which delayed her radiation treatment. Then in the middle of Kita's radiation treatments, she developed bronchitis, and she had to take a two-week break from radiation therapy.

Despite all of these challenges, Kita never sought out a formal support group. Instead, she networked with her own group of people. The very same week that Kita was diagnosed with breast cancer, two of her friends were also diagnosed. The three of them leaned on each other for support. They also shared information about treatments. The three friends became their own loving support group.

Kita was also an active member of her church. She was grateful for her "church family's" support and prayers.

"My husband, George, also helped me out in so many ways," Kita said.

George went along with Kita to all of her doctor's appointments, treatments, and procedures. He took over all of the domestic duties around the house, such as cooking and cleaning.

Kita's two children, Janna, 42, and Ryan, 37, live out of state, but they still supported her from a distance. Between Kita's loving family, friends, church, and community, she had plenty of people to lean on.

On the day of Kita's diagnosis, her life changed profoundly. She went from being an active senior who did aerobics three times a week to a warrior who needed to focus all of her strength and energy on battling cancer. Because Kita had to go to so many doctor's appointments and treatments, she didn't have a lot of time in her life left for the recreational activities she had so loved. Her journey with cancer took up a lot of her time—and energy.

Kita knew that she needed to slow down her pace and take time to take better care of herself. The one activity that Kita continued throughout her treatment was going to her quilting group. She chose to make time for that because many of the women in the group had struggled with breast cancer too. Kita's "quilting friends" were more people to support her, with whom to talk about her experiences with cancer.

Today, Kita has completed all of her radiation treatments. She's still on a maintenance drug called anastrozole (Arimidex). This drug controls levels of the hormones that were responsible for her cancer.

Like many women, Kita learned a lot from her experience with breast cancer, but the most important point was the reinforcement of having regular mammograms.

"I believe my life-long diligence to having annual mammograms saved my life," Kita said.

Now retired in Ocala, Florida, Kita is happily back to enjoying her active pre-cancer life.

Believing that Things Will Be Okay

In the early 2000s, Kristie Pinczok, 48, a direct support professional who lives in Hellertown, Pennsylvania, was a self-described "pain in the butt."

And to this day, she's glad.

Here's why.

In 2000, Kristie had two small children. She was enjoying her third pregnancy when she noticed her thyroid disorder flaring up again.

The thyroid is a gland at the base of the throat near the trachea (windpipe). Shaped like a butterfly, a healthy thyroid is a little larger than a quarter, and it usually cannot be felt through the skin. The thyroid uses iodine, which is a mineral found in some foods and in iodized salt, to help make several hormones. Thyroid hormones control heart rate, body temperature, the rate at which food is changed into energy, and the level of calcium in the blood.

"I'd had a thyroid disorder on and off for many years, Kristie said. "But while I was pregnant with my younger son, things really felt off."

Kristie's doctor kept checking her thyroid hormone levels, but nothing seemed wrong.

But Kristie couldn't shake the nagging feeling that something just wasn't right. She persisted in finding an answer to the symptoms that weren't going away. It's a good thing she did. Her persistence likely saved her life.

At Kristie's urging, her doctor finally agreed to send her for an ultrasound of her thyroid.

During Kristie's ultrasound, the ultrasound technician discovered nodules on her thyroid, which are actually a common finding. Nodules are solid or fluid-filled lumps, and the great majority of these nodules aren't problematic. As Kristie later learned, only a small percentage of thyroid nodules are cancerous. Still, the doctor agreed to send Kristie for a biopsy.

"I just felt that something was going on," Kristie said.

After the ultrasound, the radiologist zeroed in on one very small nodule for biopsy. It was barely one millimeter in diameter. The pathologist and team looked at tissue samples under the microscope 11 times. Kristie asked the professionals why they were checking so many times.

"My doctor said, 'We found several different types of cells, so we need enough of each type so we can be sure,'" Kristie remembered.

Two weeks later, the results were in.

"The doctor said that they found abnormal cells and that they thought it was cancer," Kristie said. "I just asked, 'What's the next step?' The doctor told me that they could go in and remove the nodules, both on the right side, or that they could take out half of my thyroid gland."

Kristie's doctor suggested that Kristie keep half of her thyroid because he believed that the remaining tissue would help normalize her thyroid levels. But he acknowledged that if this plan didn't work, they would have to operate again.

Kristie can smile about it now.

"I told the doctor, 'If you're in there already, take the whole thing!'" Kristie said.

The operation took place in the late spring of 2003.

The standard post-surgery pathology showed that Kristie had two types of thyroid cancer. As Kristie began to come out of anesthesia, she could hear her then-husband and her sister, a nurse, talking about what to tell her.

"I was answering in my head, but I thought I was talking back to them," Kristie recalled. When Kristie regained full consciousness, she asked, "What do you need to tell me?" Her then-husband told her that it was thyroid cancer, and it had spread to her lymph nodes.

Kristie's sister told her to pray for it to be one of the two most common types of thyroid cancer: papillary or follicular, because those two types are known to be the most curable. Kristie soon learned that it was papillary with a follicular variant. Her sister was relieved.

"That type is ridiculously easy to get rid of—compared with the other types," she told Kristie.

As if this news wasn't already a lot to cope with, this all transpired just 10 days before Kristie's sister's wedding.

Kristie underwent the surgery. Immediately afterward, she was prescribed levothyroxine sodium (Synthroid), which is a synthetic thyroid hormone replacement that's generally taken for life. Kristie also had to prepare for radioactive iodine (RAI) therapy.

RAI is taken by mouth. It collects in any remaining thyroid tissue left behind after surgical removal, including thyroid cancer cells that might have spread to other places in the body. Because only thyroid

> *"Early detection is key. And if I hadn't found my lump early, I don't know what would have been. I am still here, and I want to encourage women to do that on a regular basis."*
>
> —OLIVIA NEWTON JOHN

tissue takes up iodine, the RAI destroys both thyroid tissue and thyroid cancer cells without harming other tissue.

Before a person can begin RAI, there's an important preparation phase. Six weeks before the treatment begins, patients begin a very strict zero sodium diet.

Like probably all people who endure RAI, Kristie found that very challenging.

"I've always been someone who eats healthy, but it wasn't easy," Kristie said. "I had to be scrupulous about avoiding salt. That meant eating no meat at all. I could only eat rice and vegetables. I couldn't even drink milk—because the cow could have eaten something salty. Coffee Mate doesn't make a good milk substitute on the diet's allowance of Frosted MiniWheats."

Kristie remembers having one particular craving.

"I kept thinking that I wanted to have Papa John's thin crust pizza with mushrooms and green peppers as soon as I was done!" she said.

That would have to be put on hold until she finished the RAI—a very intensive treatment that would last a few days and require some very unusual changes to her life because of the risk of exposure to radioactive iodine.

"They won't admit you to the hospital to do the RAI," Kristie said. "So everyone in my house had to leave—even my pets!"

One hot, muggy August weekend in 2003, Kristie hunkered down in her bedroom from Friday through Sunday.

"Any body fluid had to be triple flushed in the toilet," Kristie said. "Showers were out. If I had sneezed and some of the mist from the sneeze landed on a rug, the rug would then have to be rolled up and put in storage for six months. I tried not to sneeze, or even sweat, on anything. I basically spent the entire weekend cleaning everything around me, laying on old blankets and sheets."

Once Kristie had completed the RAI, the medical team assessed her levels. Because the levels were still higher than the team would have preferred, she had to repeat the treatment a few months later.

Through it all, Kristie looked deep inside herself for strength.

"I kept thinking, 'I am so beating this!'" Kristie said.

In Kristie's typically modest style, she downplays the cancer.

"I don't consider myself to be any sort of warrior," Kristie said. "I look at so, so many other people who have gone through much worse than I did. They deserve many more accolades than me. I often tell people, 'If you're going to have cancer, this is the one to have.'"

Kristie doesn't believe that cancer affected the trajectory of her life at all.

"You define yourself, really," Kristie said. "I don't think you should let anyone or anything define who you are. I wasn't going to give the cancer any more of my life than it had already taken."

Kristie brought this same pragmatic approach to communicating with her children, a 24-year-old daughter, 22 and 17-year-old sons.

"I'm a very honest person, and I've never been one to lie to my kids," Kristie said. "In a very matter-of-fact way, I told them, 'Mommy has this cancer, so no salt for Mommy!' I remember my kids returning from their weekend away during my RAI treatment. I told them, 'Hey, I got to watch TV all weekend!'"

Although Kristie *was* honest, she did protect her kids from the harshest realities of her cancer treatments.

"I was truthful with them, but years later I told them how sick I really was," Kristie said. Unquestionably, there were some long-term effects of the RAI.

"My digestive system hasn't been great since the treatment," Kristie noted.

Like some other types of cancer, the risk for thyroid cancer can be inherited. Thankfully, Kristie's children are healthy. Only her daughter shows any sign of thyroid trouble, though Kristie's sister also had half of her thyroid gland removed.

Going through cancer and treatments has a lasting impact on most people. Kristie comments that thyroid cancer helped reinforce her commitment to health and to clean eating.

"Because there are so many things to which my body just reacts immediately, I try not to introduce anything new into the food or products I consume," Kristie said. "I really try to eat as organically as possible. I love gardening because I can control how the fruit and vegetables I consume are grown. Also, I haven't touched artificial sweeteners in 10 years," Kristie said.

Still, Kristie understands her limits. "Every now and then you have to have McDonald's french fries. You just have to."

With each passing year, Kristie knows it's less and less likely that the cancer will recur. She's grateful to share her story.

"I hope it can bring some comfort to someone," Kristie said. "I'm a big believer that things will be okay."

Enjoying Her Life–Again

Julie Reagan was a healthy 71-year-old woman who had just retired after dedicating 48 years of her life as a licensed clinical social worker. She lived and worked in Castle Rock, Colorado.

Julie's career was focused in a hospital setting, helping patients and their families. With her background in health care, she had a solid knowledge of breast cancer and its treatments.

This year, when she went in for her yearly mammogram screening, she learned she had breast cancer.

"I was somewhat anxious about losing my hair," Julie remembered. "I also was worried about the possibility of a total mastectomy. Because my mother had gone through the same thing, I was familiar with what might happen."

Julie knew the importance of treating cancer immediately, so she saw an oncologist and a surgeon right away. She felt confident in the team of medical practitioners she had selected and knew she was in good hands.

It's important to have confidence in the doctors and the hospital you are working with when you are battling cancer. It's true the sooner you get started with your treatment is essential to a good prognosis, but it is also important to trust your treatment team. Don't be afraid to seek out a second opinion.

Julie's treatment involved a partial mastectomy with lymph node involvement, three chemotherapy treatments, and six weeks of radiation.

Cancer treatments, especially when cancer is detected early, are often tolerated well. Julie had a positive experience with her treatments.

"I tolerated the treatments well, and I even was able to take daily walks," Julie said. "I lost my appetite, but I still gained weight due to my appetite for bread."

In many cases the fear of a cancer diagnosis can cause men and women to avoid recommended screening tests for cancer; however, many cancers caught early, improve your prognosis, and also require patients have less invasive and shorter treatment times.

Luckily for Julie she had a terrific support system in her husband and two adult children. She also had a great group of friends, and one of them was going through stage 4-breast cancer herself. The two friends leaned on each other as they were going through a similar struggle.

Because Julie had breast cancer patients almost daily when she was a social worker at the hospital, she was also familiar with the disease, its treatment options, potential complications, and which questions to ask her doctors. All the years of helping others came back full circle to help her through her struggle.

Today, Julie is finished with her treatments. She's enjoying her life just as it was pre-cancer.

"Having cancer hasn't really changed my life," Julie said.

"We continue to travel both internationally and domestically as well as to camp, hike, exercise at the recreational center and volunteer at the domestic violence shelter."

Most importantly she still gets her yearly mammogram.

"I recommend and encourage other women to do the same," Julie said.

Part 2

FINDING YOUR VILLAGE

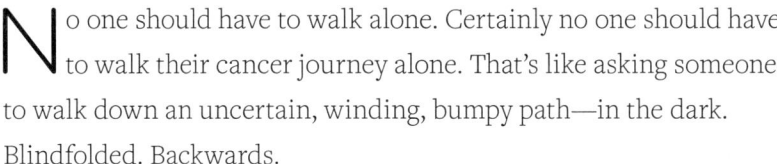

No one should have to walk alone. Certainly no one should have to walk their cancer journey alone. That's like asking someone to walk down an uncertain, winding, bumpy path—in the dark. Blindfolded. Backwards.

Cancer wreaks havoc on your body, and it also wreaks havoc on your mind and spirit. Having support can increase your quality of life by easing anxiety, lessening stress, and relieving depression.

Support can also boost your mood, self-image, and your feelings of control. Having a good friend or loving family member around can cheer you when you're down, wipe away your tears, and maybe even gift you with precious moments of normalcy—when cancer fades so far into the background of your life that you forget it's even there.

And to be practical—supportive family and friends can drive you to treatments, be a second set of ears at the doctor's, pick up groceries, fold laundry, and prepare meals. They can shoulder some of the burden of your suddenly over-full, maybe even over-whelming life.

Hopefully you have a great support team. Ideally your spouse or life partner, parents, siblings, friends—the people closest to you—will rally around you and support you emotionally, spiritually, and physically by assisting with day-to-day needs.

But sadly, not everyone is able to rise in the face of adversity. If you don't have a strong support network—or if you find your friends and family lacking, as sadly some people struggling with cancer do—create your own support team.

One thing to consider is joining a support group. Here you'll find support among people who are also fighting cancer, or who have won their battles. It can be very helpful to talk with other peoples in a similar situation who will understand what you're going through. Support from others who understand can help to improve your ability to cope, increase your ability to feel more in control over your situation, and give you a sense of hope.

You can likely find support groups at your local hospital. Also, the Cancer Support Community offers information on its website, www.cancersupportcommunity.org, and they offer more than 200 locations nationwide.

At times, you might not feel up to going to a group. Or leaving the house. Or even getting out of your pajamas. Luckily, a group can come to *you*—virtually. You can find online support groups, even groups tailored to a particular age, location, or type of cancer.

Online groups can be especially helpful for people in rural areas, those who are too ill to attend meetings in person, or those without access to transportation. It's also a plus that online support groups provide anonymity. They're available to you 24/7. Look for online support groups that are offered by knowledgeable, skilled staff from reputable organizations.

In addition to the person fighting cancer needing support, the people supporting him or her need support as well. A cancer diagnosis has a tremendous ripple effect. It affects those closest to you too. Experts estimate that 20 to 30 percent of spouses or partners of people with cancer suffer mood disturbances or even psychological impairment after a loved one's diagnosis.

Find your village, or build one.

Navigating a Bump in His Road

In 1992, John Richard Bright's life was stable. His two daughters had graduated from college. One was a lieutenant in the army. The other was a teacher. His career was winding down. He could see retirement on the horizon. A blissful quiet future appeared to stretch out before him.

The day that Richard's doctor told him he had prostate cancer took him completely by surprise.

Richard, now 85 and a retired Mack Trucks office worker in Allentown, Pennsylvania, listened patiently while the doctor outlined his options. Watchful waiting? Okay. Surgery? Not okay.

Richard was tempted to just roll the dice. Really, he just wanted to put his head in the sand and not hear the word "cancer" ever again. He didn't want to have the surgery, with the possibility of bladder incontinence for life—or worse.

But Richard's older daughter, Jennifer, wasn't letting it go that easily. Over and over, she relentlessly asked him to have the surgery.

"Family is not the most important thing. It is everything."

—MICHAEL J. FOX

She begged. She cajoled. She even resorted to bribery. Richard's "village" wasn't ready to let him go.

Finally Richard agreed.

After the surgery, Richard's recovery went well. He didn't need to have any chemotherapy or radiation. Life settled back into a comfortable groove.

One thing that Richard—and his daughters—credit with his recovery and resumed good health was his wife's sweeping dietary changes. Before it was even vogue to do so, Richard's wife, Mary, changed his diet to improve his health. She switched to a largely plant-based diet. Meat became more of a condiment than the focus of their meals.

Another change that Mary made was ramping up the amount of lycopene-rich foods she served, like spaghetti sauce. Fortunately, Richard liked pasta with sauce, because they began to eat it quite often! Lycopene is a naturally occurring pigment in food that gives fruits and vegetables—including tomatoes, watermelon, and pink grapefruit—their red color. It's a powerful antioxidant that's being studied by scientists for its possible role in helping to prevent cancer by protecting cells from damage.

Now, more than 24 years later, Richard is living comfortably in a personal care home, surrounded by a new "family" of friends and caretakers who love him. Cancer turned out to be just a bump in the road of his life. Richard has enjoyed two decades of that blissful quiet retirement—with hopefully still a few more miles yet to travel.

Accepting Help–and Love–from Family and Friends

A few years ago, Francyn Chomic and her husband moved to Appleton, Wisconsin, from Michigan. Francyn had taken the year off, and now she was looking forward to going back to work. Her son and daughter had graduated college.

By all accounts, life for Francyn was good. Things were falling into place. She was making new friends, going to dog shows, and enjoying her new life in Wisconsin.

Francyn even found a great new job as an administrative assistant. But two weeks after landing that job, Francyn found out that she had cancer.

Francyn had noticed that her left foot and ankle were swollen. In fact, they were swollen to the point that she wasn't able to wear her regular shoes. Francyn had to buy slip-on shoes. Fortunately, Francyn wasn't in any pain. But clearly something wasn't right.

Francyn knew that she needed medical attention, and so she contacted her doctor. She was able to quickly have a visit with the physician's assistant (PA). Initially, the PA diagnosed Francyn with a blood clot. Because Francyn has diabetes, it was especially critical to keep a close eye on it.

The PA advised Francyn to have an ultrasound of her leg. On the lymph nodes in her groin, the experts saw some clusters. After that, Francyn had a CT scan. Her doctor referred her to a surgeon.

"I had absolutely no family history of cancer," Francyn said.

When the surgeon showed her the results of her CT scan, he explained that he thought she had lymphoma. He scheduled her to have a biopsy.

On May 20, 2016, the surgeon called Francyn.

"You have stage 4 metastatic melanoma," he told Francyn. "It's in your lymph nodes."

"My world literally turned upside down," Francyn said. "It was devastating."

The surgeon explained that melanoma can never be completely cured. People who have it have to be tested regularly.

Upon receiving the diagnosis and prognosis, Francyn felt overwhelmed.

"I honestly couldn't believe that it was truly happening to me," Francyn said.

She and her husband had raised two children. They had spent 30 years together. They had been looking forward to enjoying each other now.

"I felt so many emotions," Francyn said. "I didn't feel much anger. But quite often, I had to make an effort to take deep breaths and to deal with each day as it came."

Francyn met with four different oncologists, who all said the same thing. Her type of cancer couldn't be removed by surgery. And it wouldn't respond to radiation. So they recommended immunotherapy.

> *"The greatest healing therapy is friendship and love."*
>
> —HUBERT H. HUMPHREY

Francyn explains that with immunotherapy, instead of putting toxins in your body, doctors hyper motivate your own white blood cells.

Vast sweeping changes came to Francyn's life. She had to stop working at the new job she had just started and enjoyed. After three months and a hospitalization, it was determined the immunotherapy didn't work, so the next course of treatment was chemotherapy. Side effects included the need for blood and magnesium transfusions, four days a week.

Francyn started a CaringBridge page, which her husband took over, posting updates every Friday. At CaringBridge.org, you can set up personal, protected websites to keep family and friends updated on a loved one's diagnosis and treatment.

Francyn's friends from her former home in Michigan sent her packages filled with love. They sent mementos, prayer shawls, and hats. Other friends sent love-filled cards. Still other friends brought Francyn and her husband meals.

"The amount of love and support I received was incredible," Francyn said. "Two of the greatest blessings were when people told me that I was going to beat cancer and when they told me that I'm an inspiration to them."

As Francyn started to feel better and regain her strength, she wanted to find a way to cheer herself up and also to give back. She began making bracelets. She has been designing bracelets to match her work outfits, so she decided to make bracelets to send to people who are battling cancer. The bracelets matched the color designated to the type of cancer they were battling. This is her way of giving back.

Although Francyn doesn't have a lot of energy, she and her husband have found a new level of love. They've booked a European cruise to celebrate her husband's birthday, their 30th wedding anniversary, and the one-year anniversary of her cancer diagnosis. Both Francyn and her husband enjoy spending time with their one-year-old grandson.

Today, Francyn can look back with great pride on how far she's come on her cancer journey.

"I don't see myself as just a success story," Francyn said. "I see myself as a warrior. And now I am sure to relish each moment of life."

Traversing Her Meandering Path

For Susan Price, of Ocklawaha, Florida, life was full. Very full. Overly full.

Susan was coming out of a very deep depression when she got her cancer diagnosis. She had so much going on and so many people to care for—her husband, three kids, grandchildren, and clients at her editing job. On top of that, Susan was dealing with her husband's issues with Asperger's syndrome.

But you never know when a challenge is actually a blessing in disguise.

"I believe that my illness 'woke up' my husband," Susan said. "Today, we have the best marriage I could imagine."

But the initial shock of being diagnosed with cancer was overwhelming.

"I was so freaked out that I didn't know which way was up," Susan said.

Before her diagnosis, Susan had been concerned about how her breast looked. She Googled a description, and she came across a picture of a breast with cancer. Immediately, Susan thought that her breast looked a lot like the breast in that photo. Exactly like the breast in that photo.

Although Susan was worried, she didn't seek medical attention right away. She knew she needed to have her breast examined by a physician, but she put it off. And then she put it off some more.

"Mom, you need to go somewhere now!" her daughter insisted.

Finally, Susan's daughter's urging prompted her to seek medical help.

Susan's cancer journey was a meandering one. She did go somewhere for medical help—to the chiropractor where her daughter works. The chiropractor examined Susan, and she shared with Susan what she found.

"I have never seen a more perfect example of breast cancer," the chiropractor said.

Susan next made connections through her church. She discussed her recent suspicion with a priest in her congregation. That priest, in turn, told Susan about a parishioner who was a surgeon. Susan met the surgeon, and that would be the doctor who would soon perform the surgery.

Susan had questions. So many questions. Of her doctors. Even of God.

"God, why did you let this happen to me?" Susan asked. "I had no reason to have cancer." At least, no reason that she thought of.

But as time went on, Susan began to learn about various factors that can contribute to cancer that no one had ever told her, such as stress. In fact, Susan started to realize there was *much* about cancer she previously had no idea about. Since then, Susan has become a firm believer in how truly important it is to see your doctor on a regular basis.

"You never know where a blessing can come from."

—TEENA MARIE

"I learned so much as this new chapter of my life unfolded," Susan said.

Susan also found that there was much to *deal* with upon learning she had cancer. Susan tried to wrap her head around this new situation, and at the same time, her husband struggled with it as well. Susan said that for her husband, it was a long trip. Naturally, he meant well and was trying to be helpful. Eventually, the pieces came together. Initially, however, there were many unknowns.

"We just didn't have all the details," Susan said.

Susan did gain some comfort in meeting her surgeon, whom she liked very much. Susan really appreciated her comforting demeanor. The surgeon invited Susan to call her anytime, and that was very reassuring. The idea that Susan could literally reach out to talk with her doctor meant so much.

At some point, the details of Susan's diagnosis became clearer. Then a plan was put in place. Susan had surgery. Two weeks after that, she began chemotherapy and radiation.

"I didn't know anything about chemo," Susan said. "With my first treatment, I was sick, but after that, it wasn't so bad."

Susan's cancer diagnosis had a tremendous ripple effect on her life. She had to let go of her editing job. Although necessary, it was disappointing. Even though the job didn't pay a lot, Susan really enjoyed it. It was the loss of her job that caused Susan to fall apart for the first couple of weeks.

"It was too much to take," Susan said. "It all felt unreal."

Fortunately, Susan found a lot of support throughout her cancer journey. Church has been an integral part of her life.

One of Susan's daughters has a spare room in her home, and when Susan had to go to the doctor, she welcomed Susan to stay at her house. This gave Susan a quiet, comfortable place to rest after her appointments. Another daughter visited with her new baby, which Susan really looked forward to. For Susan, the love and support of her family have been so important.

If you ask Susan how she is doing today, she will admit, almost with a chuckle, that she's worried about her blood pressure. But in general, her spirits are good.

Circling Her Wagons of Friends

In the spring of 2014, Samantha Beck, 46, a middle school teacher in Philadelphia, Pennsylvania, went to her regular gynecology appointment. She chatted with her ob-gyn about their kids, vacation plans, and work.

"See you next year!" Samantha said cheerfully as she walked out of the door.

After a dozen years of stress-free, problem-free annual exams, the ob-gyn felt more like an old friend to Samantha than a physician.

"I always believed I was healthy. I always thought that my test results would be fine, and they always were," Samantha said.

Until they weren't.

A few weeks later, the nurse from the doctor's office called. The Pap test results were abnormal. The nurse instructed Samantha to come back in for a follow-up test.

I'm sure it's nothing, Samantha thought to herself.

Except it wasn't.

The follow-up Pap test was abnormal too. The ob-gyn recommended

> *Behold, I will bring it health and healing;*
> *I will heal them and reveal to them the*
> *abundance of peace and truth.*
>
> JEREMIAH 33:6

a procedure called a LEEP. Short for loop electrosurgical excision procedure, a LEEP removes abnormal tissue from the cervix by cutting it away using a thin wire loop that carries an electrical current.

"I'm sure that it will be normal," the ob-gyn said.

But it wasn't.

A few weeks later, the ob-gyn herself called. Even the doctor sounded surprised as she told Samantha the news that the LEEP had shown abnormal lesions.

"What would you do?" Samantha asked.

"You're done having children, right? I'd have a hysterectomy," the ob-gyn replied. Understanding the possible seriousness of the situation, Samantha got a referral from the ob-gyn to a nearby gynecologic oncologist. He recommended a total hysterectomy, removing her cervix, uterus, and Fallopian tubes—mainly as a precaution.

"We don't expect to find anything else," he said optimistically.

Except they did.

When Samantha returned a few weeks later to get the results, she knew that it wasn't a great sign when the doctor came into the exam room with a somber-looking nurse trailing behind.

"I'm very surprised to tell you that we found a small cancer," the doctor said. He recommended eight weeks of daily radiation and eight weeks of weekly chemotherapy. School had just let out for the summer. The treatments would take up almost every single week of her family's precious summer break.

The first thought in Samantha's mind was, *How am I going to make my kids go to the hospital with me every single day of their entire summer?* Her boys were nine and seven years old at the time. The simple answer was, *I can't.*

The next few days were a blur of emotions, fears, and worries. When Samantha returned to the doctor's office a few days later to schedule her treatment appointments, the full impact of the time commitment hit home. It took about a half hour to drive to the hospital, around an hour to wait for and receive the treatments, and then another half hour to drive back home. Samantha scheduled her appointments for early afternoons, trying to minimize the disruption to the family's schedule.

She looked around the doctor's office for a solution. Oncology waiting rooms aren't designed with school-aged kids in mind! There was nowhere safe for her kids to wait alone while she received her treatments. Truth be told, though, she didn't really *want* to drag them along even if it was possible. Samantha imagined that there would be plenty of days ahead where her emotions would be high and her nerves would be frayed. She didn't want to expose her kids to that.

To make matters worse, Samantha's marriage had been on shaky ground for many months before. She couldn't ask her husband to miss work to drive her to and from the daily appointments.

Clearly, she needed help. Fortunately, she didn't have to look far to find it.

Samantha reached out to several close friends to see if they could watch her kids while she went to her treatments. As a wonderful bonus, those friends' children were also her kids' friends. When they heard her story, friend after friend responded that they would be happy to help.

Just a few hours and phone calls later, Samantha created a schedule: One friend promised to watch the boys every Monday, two friends split Tuesdays, another two friends took Wednesdays, Samantha's parents took Thursdays, and another friend took Fridays. A plan had come together—effortlessly!

As the summer went on, week stretched on to week. Day after day, Samantha dropped her boys off at their friends' houses for afternoon playdates. The kids had a wonderful summer, packed with joy-filled, fun-filled playdates. They didn't feel that their summer was ruined—if anything, it was enhanced!

After a long summer of treatments, more than 40 trips to the hospital, and countless hours of meditation and prayer, Samantha holds one very happy memory from it all. She remembers all of the help and kindness that was so freely and generously offered by a strong, loving circle of friends.

"When my doctor told me I had cancer, he said, 'This is going to change you in many ways. And they won't all be bad,'" Samantha remembers. "And he was right."

Finding Support in a City Rich with Help

April Salvant, 44, a mother of five children, has dedicated her life to helping others. For four years, her family did missionary work in Haiti, running an orphanage.

In 2015, the family came back to the United States for a visit. During the visit, April and her children had their routine doctors' appointments.

"I felt that God was sending me a strong message to make sure I went for my mammogram," April said.

That's when April learned that she had a type of breast cancer called stage 1 invasive ductal carcinoma.

It was a blessing that April followed up. She needed immediate surgery and chemotherapy. Even though the surgeon didn't recommend a double mastectomy, April had one anyway, with full support from her treatment team. Her cancer was driven by three hormones estrogen, progesterone, and HER2. This is referred to in the medical community as a triple positive cancer.

Although a double mastectomy is far more invasive than a lumpectomy, April knew that it would substantially lower her risk of recurring cancers. There were a lot of surgeries, chemotherapy treatments, and bumps in the road to follow.

During one of April's reconstructive surgeries, she suffered from an infection and became ill. In addition, because hormones worsened April's cancer, she needed to take drugs to put her into early menopause. She was prescribed Tamoxifen (Nolvadex) to do this, but it caused her to have a stroke during the course of her treatment. She then had to be put into menopause by having a oophorectomy and was put on Femara (an estrogen blocker for post menopausal women). But the Femara caused debilitating bone pain so she switched to Arimidese which will hopefully have fewer side effects. Thankfully, the side effects from the stroke were minimal, and she was able to continue living a normal life.

Along with all of these physical challenges, April knew it would be wise to move back to the United States. She chose to return to Richmond, Virginia, where her church was located and she and her family had lived previously.

"We were so blessed to be returning to such a welcoming and benevolent community," April said. "We moved back from Haiti with only six suitcases. We had no furniture, cooking utensils, or dishes."

The family moved so quickly that most of their children didn't even get to say goodbye to their friends abroad. Only April, her husband, and one of their children returned to Haiti to close up their home and gather their belongings.

The Richmond community pulled together to make sure the family had all the essentials needed for everyday living. They donated furniture, pots and pans, rugs, and basic home furnishings. Neighbors and church members brought the family meals and

> *"Walking with a friend in the dark is better than walking alone in the light."*
>
> —HELEN KELLER

offered to give the children rides to school events and activities. One of April's friends held a Go Fund Me fundraiser for her online, raising more than $50,000 to help out with expenses.

April looked for a support group to join. She couldn't find quite the right one.

"It's important to find a support group that meets your needs and feels 'right' to you," April said. "Don't give up on looking for a support group just because the first one wasn't a perfect fit. It's okay to keep looking."

April finally found her group: Beyond Boobs. This organization focuses on women with breast cancer aged 50 and younger. Beyond Boobs (www.beyondboobs.com) offers networking and medical referrals to their members. Members of Beyond Boobs refer to themselves as "Boobers," and the group goes on weekend retreats together. During these retreats there are activities, massages, healthy meals, and lectures. Most importantly, breast cancer survivors are able to relate to each other in a relaxed environment. They share their problems and struggles, and they also share their celebrations and triumphs.

April has used her connections with her support group and her community to make healthy lifestyle changes.

"I found that a lot of people going through cancer adopt healthier eating and exercising habits," April said. "In my experience, doctors don't offer much advice on healthy eating."

Through April's research and conversations with other patients, she started eating a more organic diet. In the beginning, she was extremely strict with her consumption of *only* organic foods. This made eating out and dining at friends' houses very difficult. It's also expensive to feed a family of seven all organic food!

So April found a compromise. She buys local lean meats, and she tries to eat as many organic vegetables and fruits as possible.

Because one of April's friends is a Lemongrass Spa consultant, April also switched to chemical-free and natural personal care products. She uses Lemongrass Spa natural organic deodorants, shampoos, and skin care products.

"I especially avoid all parabens," April said.

April's breast cancer diagnosis, treatments, and surgeries, coupled with the family's international relocation, put them all through many difficult challenges. All seven family members are courageous, caring, and brave. They worked so hard in Haiti to give people there a better life. Their benevolence was reciprocated when they returned to Richmond, Virginia, needing help through April's illness.

When April was first diagnosed, she was terrified not to be established in a community in the United States. She wondered: *Where will I seek out the right doctors? Who will help carpool the children when I'm not feeling well?* These questions and more went through her mind, but the community of Richmond quickly put her fears to rest—stepping in to help out in any way needed.

Sometimes it takes a village. And April and her family found one.

Growing Her Community of Support

In the small town of Cawen, West Virginia, Martha Armentrout, 57, has made a beautiful life for her husband, Larry, and their two grown children, Jennifer and David. Cawen is a close-knit community where everybody knows each other, helps each other out, and pulls together in time of need.

Before her cancer diagnosis, Martha was very active in her community. She worked in food preparation at the local elementary school, where she impacted the lives of many young students. She enjoyed when the children brought her drawings and told her stories about their day.

"That's what I miss the most," Martha said.

She also misses being able to take care of her family and playing with her grandson Warren, 8. Cancer has taken a lot from Martha, but it hasn't taken away her tenacity to survive, her ability to laugh, and her faith in God and her community.

On February 1, 2016, Martha and her husband had spent the day in Morgantown, West Virginia, visiting her ill brother-in-law at the hospital. It had been a long and stressful day, and Martha attributed her exhaustion to the marathon day she had completed.

But even after Martha and her husband were back home, she still didn't feel right. As time went on, Martha's stomach became more and more upset. Martha called to her husband to help her to the bathroom. But before he could get to her, she collapsed to the floor.

Martha's husband called 911 for help, and she regained consciousness. Before emergency services arrived, though, Martha collapsed again. At the time, her husband and daughter thought she was simply fainting.

That night at the emergency room, the doctors couldn't find anything wrong with Martha, so they directed her to follow up with her family physician. After her family doctor ordered an MRI (magnetic resonance imaging) scan of her brain, the radiologist discovered the dark shadow of a brain tumor. It turns out the "fainting" episodes were actually seizures.

Martha was sent to a specialist in Morgantown for treatment. She was diagnosed with a glioblastoma, an aggressive type of brain cancer. Glioblastoma tumors are extremely difficult to remove because they often grow tentacles that wrap themselves around the brain.

The part of the brain most affected by Martha's tumor was the area controlling her ability to express emotions. Because of this, when Martha found out about her tumor, she was unable to express sadness. She was only able to sit and watch her family's overwhelming reaction of grief. The cancer had affected the part of her brain that experiences emotion.

Martha's treatment started with surgery to remove as much of the tumor as possible. Unfortunately, her tumor couldn't be completely removed because of the tentacles that had intertwined themselves around parts of her brain. After the surgery, Martha needed radiation and chemotherapy. Her doctors were also fighting this cancer with a new treatment called Optune, which attacks the cancer with alternating electronic fields. Specifically designed patches were placed on Martha's head to transmit the electronic waves. Her head was shaved in order for the patches to make good contact, and the patches were replaced every few days. A caretaker at home was able to apply the new patches by following a diagram drawn by the physician.

After only two months of treatments, Martha's tumor had shrunk to half its original size. This was great news for the family because this type of cancer can never be cured. It can only be kept under control through treatment, and thankfully, Martha's cancer is responding well to this new treatment option.

During all of her treatments, Martha had the support of her dedicated family. Her husband, Larry, and daughter, Jennifer, have been by her side as her primary caretakers. They both selflessly dedicate themselves to keeping Martha safe and comfortable. She is no longer able to prepare meals for the family or even get up and take a shower by herself. Larry and Jennifer have taken over all these duties—and more—to help Martha through this difficult time.

Martha's son, David, who lives in a neighboring county, also is an invaluable source of support. For Mother's Day last year, he decided against buying cut flowers. Instead he brought his tractor over to her house, tilled the front flower bed, and planted wildflowers for his mother to enjoy all summer long.

David also brings his son, Warren, over to visit with his grandmom.

"Warren's visits are the highlight of my day," Martha said. "He's only eight years old, but he has the maturity to comprehend what is going on."

> *"A real friend is one who walks in when the rest of the world walks out."*
>
> —WALTER WINCHELL

Warren offers compassion for and distractions from the struggle his grandmom is going through. He always asks her how she is feeling and is quick to bring out a joke to make her laugh. Laughter is such a welcome distraction and an effective tool in the arsenal against cancer. Martha's doctor's last name is Gonzales, so Warren asked his grandmom, "Do you know what your doctor's first name is? It's Speedy—he's Speedy Gonzales!"

Martha laughed, and she never forgot her doctor's name again.

Along with Martha's family, the caring and intimate community of Cawen, West Virginia has also helped and supported Martha through her journey with cancer. Before she became ill, she was always helping out with local fundraisers. A lot of these fundraisers were to support people with cancer. Because her career was in food services, Martha was happy to donate her talent and time to help prepare dinners for these events. She has done numerous fundraisers to help others in this capacity, so it wasn't a surprise when the community held a fundraiser for her.

Staff members from the elementary school where she worked also continue to reach out to her. One day, the secretary at the school stopped by to see how she was doing. The teachers and staff are always expressing how much they miss her at work and hope that she will be well enough to return soon.

Martha is feeling much better these days with her brain tumor shrinking. She maintains a positive attitude and good sense of humor despite all she has been through. At this point her doctors are able to successfully manage her disease, and she is looking forward to becoming stronger and more active again.

"I'm so grateful to my friends and family," Martha said.

And, with the return of spring, she can't wait to plant flowers with her grandson.

Part 3

KEEPING THE FAITH IN GOD— AND MEDICINE

What do you do when you feel like you've been swept off of your feet by a giant, swirling, terrifying tornado? Reach out and find something to hold onto for dear life.

For many people battling cancer, that something to hold on to is faith. That might be faith in God, or the universe, or all that is good and right in the world. It can be intensely comforting to find strength in a higher power—in something much greater than we are.

According to the U.S. Centers for Disease Control and Prevention (CDC), 69 percent of people with cancer say they pray for their health.

It turns out that might be an excellent idea: A recent study published in *Cancer*, a peer-reviewed journal of the American Cancer Society, suggests a link between religious or spiritual beliefs and better physical health reported among patients with cancer.

For the report, researchers from Moffitt Cancer Center in Tampa, Florida, looked at the results of several published studies on the topic, which included more than 32,000 cancer patients combined. The researchers found a link between patients with higher levels of spiritual well-being and better physical health. The researchers did not look at whether spiritual well-being affected patient survival or cancer recurrence, however.

While some people look to their faith for strength, others look to medicine. They might revere at their medical team with confidence

> ## *"Feed your faith, and your fears will starve to death."*
>
> —ANONYMOUS

in their training, abilities, and skills. They could trust and believe in the power of modern medicine to heal.

These beliefs have long-standing, time-tested value. We hold many powerful images of the medical profession dear: from old-time doctors making house calls to today's confident physicians with vast knowledge and resources at their fingertips.

No matter which you find strength in—God, medicine, or both—find the strength you *can*, and find it you *will*.

Attracting Positivity and Hope

When Heidi Sprankle, 46, a stay-at-home mom in Pottstown, PA, had her first abnormal Pap test, she thought it was a fluke. The second one got her attention. But it didn't get her down.

"I literally refused to think anything negative," Heidi said. "I was determined to be positive."

Being positive had helped Heidi through some rough times in life—divorce, miscarriage, job changes. Over the years, Heidi had read a lot about the law of attraction, which simply means what you focus on is what comes to be. If you worry about bad things happening, they are more likely to happen. You attract bad things to your life. On the other hand, if you think about good things, you're more likely to attract good things to your life. What you think about, you bring about.

As Heidi waited to have the loop electrosurgical excision procedure (LEEP) that her doctor recommended, she thought to herself, *I am healthy* and *My body is taking care of this.*

"I visualized the bad cells exiting my body," she said.

"It's really important that you feel good. Because this feeling good is what goes out as a signal into the universe and starts to attract more of itself to you. So the more you can feel good, the more you will attract the things that help you feel good and that will keep bringing you up higher and higher."

—JOE VITALE

When Heidi's doctor came into the recovery room after the procedure, Heidi wasn't surprised at all to hear her say, "Everything looked great!" However, the doctor cautioned that she could see only what was on the *outside*. Later results from cells further inside her cervix showed abnormal cells.

"I truly believe that my LEEP procedure showed no abnormal cells outside because my body was healing—from the outside in," Heidi said. "Part of me wondered if, given enough time, my body could heal itself completely. But I wasn't going to risk my life to find out."

Heidi decided to have the recommended hysterectomy, chemotherapy, and radiation.

When Heidi scheduled her treatments, the nurse showed an entire PowerPoint presentation about all of the bad side effects of the chemo and radiation.

"The nurse said I *would* have all of the side effects from radiation and chemo—not that I *might* have them," Heidi said. "I was determined that I was not going to have them, and I didn't."

From her first treatment, Heidi began to use the law of attraction. This takes practice and consistency, but it can work.

One of the most common side effects of the treatments is nausea. Whenever Heidi felt nauseated, she thought to herself, *I need to feel better. I believe I feel better. I will be deeply grateful when I feel better.*

Almost like magic, a few minutes later, Heidi *did* feel better. Every. Single. Time.

"I might have done this 2,000 times a day," Heidi said. "But it worked."

Another common side effect of the radiation is skin problems, such as rashes. Every day, faithfully, Heidi slathered on a calendula cream the doctor had recommended. As she put it on her skin, she thought to herself, *My skin is healthy and strong.*

Heidi never got a single bit of rash.

Along the same lines, when Heidi had her radiation treatments, she would lie there, surrounded by the whirring, rotating machine, imagining that magic beams of light were shooting out of the machine, targeting any bad cells with pinpoint precision. *Bam! Blast! Kapow!*

"I'm sure that every single bad cancer cell is gone," Heidi said. "They were blasted to smithereens by the law of attraction."

Finding Strength in Her "Prayer Closet"

Ann Walters, 67, found a peaceful place on her property in Laurel, Mississippi, to sit and talk to God.

Ann lives on 20 acres of land that joins with a lake. She walks down a small road through the woods to sit in a chair by a pier built by her husband, who's a minister and the associate pastor at her church.

In the past, Anne would sit out on the pier. But since her cancer had spread to her brain, she's prone to dizziness. Now Ann's afraid she'll fall, so she stays on the edge of the lake, sits, and talks to God.

"I tell God what I'm feeling," Ann said. "If I want to cry, it's like He offers me a shoulder that I can cry on."

Ann calls this special place her "prayer closet." It's somewhere that Ann can go, be alone with God, and pray.

"It's surrounded by trees," Ann said. "With the sun setting, it's beautiful. The birds are singing."

About 10 years ago, Ann had breast cancer. She needed to have a mastectomy, and she also had chemotherapy for nine months.

"During my surgery, I died on the operating table," Ann said. "I woke up to the doctors rescuitating me!"

At the time, Ann's vocal cords became paralyzed, and a tracheotomy was necessary.

Ann was cancer-free for many years. But then, two years ago, she was in the hospital for kidney stones, and an X-ray revealed the cancer had come back. This time it had spread to her bones, her brain, and her neck.

Over the past two years, Ann has had a lot of chemo and radiation, and she has lived longer than her doctor thought she would. She said she hasn't really been able to cope with chemo, but she still cooks and cleans her house. She has chemo every day for seven days followed by seven days off. On her week off, she goes to church on Sunday, but when she's taking chemo, she doesn't have the energy to get dressed and go.

Ann hasn't been able to work since the cancer came back. She used to help a woman in her eighties who had Alzheimer's disease.

The original chemo treatments haven't done much for Ann's cancer, but for the past three months, Ann's doctors have been trying a new chemo drug to see if it will help. She also takes a basket-full of medications, most over-the-counter, including calcium for her bones and melatonin to help her sleep.

"I never thought I'd do that," Ann said. "I don't like taking drugs."

When Ann's son, who's 48 and lives in Phoenix, Arizona, visited her during her radiation treatment, a nurse told him how strong and brave Ann is. But Ann brushed the comment off.

"What choice do I have, other than to keep going?" Ann said.

Her friends and family have also helped her through. Her husband,

> *"To trust God in the light is nothing.
> But trust Him in the dark—that is faith."*
>
> —C.H. SPURGEON

son, three grandchildren, sister, and sisters-in-law have given her support over the past two years. She also has friends she can rely on.

"Years ago, a preacher said that if you can count six friends who are truly friends, then you're a wealthy person," Ann said. "I thought, 'Everybody has six friends.'"

Ann thought about it some more, and she became grateful that she has so many friends who are there for her anytime she wants to pick up the phone and ask, "Can I talk or can you come over?" Her son told her she had a steady flow of people coming to visit her in the hospital.

"I just love people," Ann said.

But sometimes Ann needs a retreat to her prayer closet by the lake. That happens especially when her headaches are bad or if her right shoulder is more painful than usual and she doesn't want to take pain pills.

"I have to ask God to help me handle this," Ann said. "When you can't tell anyone else something, you can tell God."

Keeping the Faith and Confidence

In the fall of 2007, Jamie Breeden, 61, of Glen Allen, Virginia, was blessed with a fulfilling life. Jamie was working full-time as an office manager for Sweet Monday, a nonprofit women's ministry that encourages and equips women to share the gospel and reach women through friendship evangelism, and caring for her 84-year-old mother. The single mom of an adorable English setter, Hallie, Jamie had her annual mammogram just before Thanksgiving. Then she went out of town for the Thanksgiving weekend.

While Jamie was away, she got the kind of phone message from the doctor's office all women dread.

"They said they wanted me to call them back immediately—and to make plans to come into the office as soon as possible," Jamie remembered. "The first thing I did was get down on my knees to pray. I had always thought I would just give up if I got this kind of call. Instead, I found myself saying, 'Lord, I want to have a great week with my family.' I just knew it was all going to be okay."

As Jamie leaned on her faith—as she always had before in her life—she prepared for the challenges ahead.

"When I came home, the doctors ordered an ultrasound, which was followed by a stereotactic biopsy and surgery to remove cancerous calcifications and then ultimately a mastectomy," Jamie said.

But as Jamie discovered, there was even more to the story.

Doctors found that the cancer—a tumor on Jamie's chest wall—was hormone receptor-positive. This type of cancer is commonly referred to as estrogen positive. It's the most common type of breast cancer. It depends upon estrogen and/or progesterone to grow.

Armed with this new information, Jamie's oncologist prescribed five years of hormone therapy, in the form of estrogen-blocking medication. The goal of this therapy is to lower the level of estrogen in the body or at least to block the hormone from stimulating any remaining cancer cells. The logic is that if the hormones cannot get to the cancer cells, the cancer cannot use them to grow.

Like many women, Jamie elected to have breast reconstruction after her mastectomy. This involved employing a muscle expander to make room insert a breast implant. Unfortunately, the tissue around the implant became infected, and the implant had to be removed.

Despite this new challenge, Jamie's doctors continued to be optimistic about her prognosis.

"They said my type of cancer has only a 6 percent recurrence rate," Jamie said.

Heartened by this very encouraging statistic, Jamie continued to be vigilant with her mammograms and breast self-exams, which are critical for everyone. At the end of 2013, Jamie detected a lump in her breast, which led to an ultrasound followed by breast surgery in February 2014. From March to August of that year, Jamie underwent chemotherapy and radiation. At the end of the treatment, she was relieved to discover that the cancer hadn't spread to her lymph nodes.

Jamie continued to take the estrogen-blocking medication. For some women, this medicine can be extremely difficult to tolerate.

"I was sick a lot," Jamie said. "Because I had such severe joint pain, I ended up trying three different estrogen-blocking medications. In May 2016, I started Tamoxifen, but in September, I thought I had pneumonia. It turned out to be blood clots in my legs and lungs caused by Tamoxifen."

Fortunately, Jamie's medical team was able to remedy the situation after six days in the hospital. She continues to take the Tamoxifen, but she's now on blood thinners to reduce the clotting risk.

Walking through her cancer journey motivated Jamie to try to reduce the toxins in her life. She discovered Lemongrass Spa products in her quest, and she's particularly fond of Lemongrass Spa's Hair Spray with Flax Seed, the Ultra Hydrating Body Crème and Healing Elements balm.

Jamie's journey has certainly been trying, and she credits her deep faith with lifting her up in the darkest moments.

"I always thought that I would so dread cancer, but in many ways it was a gift," Jamie said. "I've met incredible people along the way, and I've been so supported by my church family and close friends."

Jamie is modest about her bravery. In the midst of her cancer recurrence, she lost two very close friends and her mother within a matter of months.

"God gave me a peace about it," Jamie said. "I knew that he would bring me through. My faith and trust in the Lord has sustained me."

In many ways, Jamie's story reflects her favorite verse of Scripture, Hebrews 11:1: "Now faith is confidence in what we hope for and assurance about what we do not see."

Working Through Her List

Back in the early 1980s, Jan Piche longed to have children.

"I was in a great relationship," Jan said. "Starting a family was my biggest dream."

But Jan's dream was snatched away from her—before she could even try to live it.

"At age 30, wham! I got hit with cervical cancer," Jan said.

That's when Jan's life went off the rails.

"My doctor never said the word 'cancer' to me," Jan said. "He didn't have to. I knew that it was. Practically everyone in my family has had cancer. My dad had lymphoma and stomach cancer, then melanoma and prostate cancer. My mom and both of my brothers died of lung cancer. Many of my aunts and uncles died of cancer too."

Jan's doctors took an aggressive stance against the cancer. Jan had a hysterectomy, six weeks of external radiation, and two radiation implants.

"I had hoped that the treatments wouldn't launch me into menopause, but they did," Jan said. "All I could think about at the time was that I would never have children. In time, I got over that disappointment because I was so grateful to be alive. I thank God every day that I'm still here."

Even though receiving a cancer diagnosis is scary and life-altering, Jan had a wonderful example to follow. In the 1970s, her dad was diagnosed with cancer. The doctor said that he had only two to three months to live.

"My dad's oncologist asked him, 'Are you a man of faith?'" Jan remembered. "When my dad said yes, the oncologist said, 'Good, because when I said two to three months, I was being optimistic.'"

Against all odds, Jan's dad vowed that he would live to see his granddaughter graduate. The catch? She had just been born!

"My dad lived for 19 more years!" Jan said. "He did get to see his granddaughter graduate. Ironically, he didn't even die from the cancer."

Jan has reflected often on her dad's longevity.

"I think that my father's attitude and his faith were half the cure," Jan said. "My dad's attitude was overwhelmingly positive. He didn't talk about cancer much. My dad kind of shrugged it off. 'I have put my faith in the Lord,' he would say."

Back in the 1980s, Jan won her battle with cervical cancer. But that wouldn't be the last time cancer would wreak havoc on her life—by far. In 2003, Jan went for her routine mammogram. Because the doctors saw calcifications, they urged her to have a biopsy. And then they found the cancer in her left breast.

Because they had caught it very early, Jan had a partial mastectomy. The cancer was determined to be HER2 positive, so she had six weeks of radiation treatments.

Just a year and a half later, it felt like déjà vu all over again when doctors found cancer in Jan's right breast. She had another partial mastectomy and six more weeks of radiation.

> *"Courage isn't having the strength to go on. It is going on when you don't have the strength."*
>
> —NAPOLEON

Then in 2007, Jan had what she thought was a pulled muscle in her chest. Her intuition told her something was wrong. Very wrong. She requested a bone scan.

The cancer had spread to her sternum. Jan's oncologist put her on cancer-inhibiting medication. The average person lives two to three years on this drug. So far, Jan has made it 9½ years.

In 2010, another mammogram found cancer again in Jan's right breast. This time, she had a bilateral mastectomy.

"Someone asked me, 'Do you feel like less of a woman now?'" Jan recalled. "I said, 'No! Even though I don't have breasts, I'm still the same person I always was!'"

Certainly, Jan has "down days," but she fights them as best she can.

"I pray to God all of the time," Jan said. "It's a miracle that through my life of cancer, I'm still here. I know that my faith in God has a lot to do with it. I keep looking back to the miracle of my dad. I know that God can do miracles. When I feel low, I pray to God and ask Him for strength. Sometimes I literally drop to my knees and pray. I ask for strength, and I thank Him for still being here.

"Whenever I start feeling down, I remind myself that there are plenty of people who have it much worse than I do," Jan said. "My oncologist calls me his poster child for survival."

One of the biggest challenges for Jan has been accepting help from other people. Fiercely independent, she sold her home after her mastectomy to simplify her life. Now she rents a condo. She prefers to go to her appointments alone, rather than asking friends or family to drive her.

Today, Jan, 63, is a retired court clerk in New York City.

"I decided life's too short. You should retire when you can," Jan said. "I created a bucket list, and I'm working through my list. So far, I've ridden in a NASCAR, gone zip-lining, swam with dolphins, and parasailed! As I cross items off of my bucket list, I keep adding more. The only thing on my list I probably won't get to do is to go tandem skydiving! But it's not for lack of wanting to!"

Drawing on Her Faith

At the age of 27 and a new mother to her son, Brody, breast cancer was the furthest thought from Amber Lemmer's mind.

One night, while Amber was getting ready for bed, something told her to check her breast. She believes it was her strong Christian faith that guided her to do a breast self-exam that night.

Amber, an employee at PNC bank, who lives in Portage, Michigan, found a lump. Immediately, she sought out a medical evaluation. Amber learned that she had a type of breast cancer that's rare for women her age called invasive ductal carcinoma.

Amber quickly recalibrated her thoughts, leaning hard on her faith to get her through what would prove to be a difficult and challenging battle with cancer. What Amber didn't know at the time was that God was also going to give her the strength to see the positives born out of her struggle.

Amber's doctors prescribed an aggressive treatment plan: a double mastectomy and reconstructive surgery along with radiation and chemotherapy treatments. It's hard enough keeping up with a toddler

> *"Courage doesn't always roar. Sometimes courage is the quiet voice at the end of the day saying 'I'll try again tomorrow.'"*
>
> —MARY ANNE RADMACHER

when you're feeling well, but doing it while undergoing surgery, chemotherapy, and radiation treatments requires almost superhuman effort.

"God always gave me friends and family to support me," Amber said.

In the beginning of Amber's chemotherapy treatment, she was given a drug called Doxorubicin (Adriamycin). This drug is informally known around the hospital as the "red devil" because it makes people so sick.

On the third day after receiving the drug, Amber would feel violently ill. Fortunately, her mother and mother-in-law lived close by and could help out with Brody. Often Amber and Brody went to her parents' house for her recovery time while her husband was at work.

Amber also needed help after her surgery. For eight weeks afterward, she wasn't allowed to pick up her son. Her family was invaluable to her during this time. Her husband was her steady rock and stepped up immensely in every aspect of daily life, making the healing process less stressful

"Reaching out to friends and family during cancer treatments is critical," Amber said. "Trying to take care of everything on your own is like begging for frustration, injury, and exhaustion."

Throughout Amber's treatment and recovery, she sought out the positives of her challenging situation. For example, Amber turned her cancer diagnosis into a teaching opportunity. Before she was diagnosed, she was an active person. She enjoyed horseback riding, 4-H club mentoring, and camping. A month after her surgery, and right after her first chemotherapy treatment, it was time for the 4-H club's annual fair. Amber knew that the kids had worked hard all year long with their animals to show off their accomplishments at this event. She made it a point to be there for the kids and help them on this important day.

"I wanted the kids to understand that life still goes on after a cancer diagnosis," Amber said. "I also wanted to ease their fears about the disease."

It takes a strong person with a lot of faith to overcome such adversity and channel it into an educational moment for others.

Amber even used the word "blessing" to describe some of the changes cancer made in her life. She always had a strong Christian faith, but her struggle with cancer made her faith even stronger. In addition to regular Sunday services, Amber and her husband became more involved in church activities such as Bible studies and a few ministry groups within the church.

"My diagnosis and treatment also gave me the chance to stay home with my son," Amber said. "This was always a dream of mine, but it didn't become a reality until cancer came into my life. God also seemed to give me just what I needed, just at the right time."

A few years prior to her cancer diagnosis, God provided an amazing horse that she was able to form a beautiful relationship with, making him perfect for Amber to ride during her illness. Amber believes that God also sent her family a lovely cat to keep her company on challenging days. The family had planned to adopt a dog, but at the shelter a special little feline caught their eye. Her dog of nine years was also a special gift from God that has seen her through many challenging days.

Today, Amber is 28 years old and feeling great. She still has some procedures ahead of her, and she will need to be monitored for any reoccurring cancer. But she is grateful to be able to enjoy horseback riding with her mother and sisters and training dogs with the 4-H club.

Living Her Life Guided by Her Faith

As a mom of eight who homeschools six of her children, Michele Perdomo, 41, relies on her strong faith and the support of her close-knit family and fellow churchgoers in Duncan, South Carolina. In the past few years, that support has been even more important in her life.

Two days before Mother's Day 2016—and a week after her husband Tony's grandmother, who lived with the family, passed away at 94—Michele learned she had stage 2 invasive breast cancer.

"I am here to serve our almighty God," Michele said. "I believe that my life is not my story. It's His."

Michele's experience with cancer began almost by accident. One night shortly after her husband's grandmother died, Michele and Tony were good-naturedly play fighting when he poked what felt like a sizeable lump in her chest.

"Michele, what's that?" Tony asked.

Michele didn't know, but because she had just turned 40 the

month before, she didn't think she should worry unnecessarily. Although statistics show one in eight women in the United States will be diagnosed with breast cancer in their lifetime, only 15 percent of all breast cancers occur in women under 45. Still, to be sure, she made an appointment for a mammogram the following Monday.

The initial results weren't good, so the doctors scheduled a biopsy for the next day and discovered the cancer. Michele's medical team also wanted to be sure the cancer wasn't genetic in nature, and they learned it was not. About 5 to 10 percent of breast cancers in America are hereditary and are caused by inherited changes in genes such as BRCA1 and BRCA2.

"I felt numb—almost like this wasn't happening," Michele remembers. "I just kept thinking about how this would affect Tony, whose own mom had passed away after a battle with cancer before we got married, and how it might impact the kids, of course."

That was just the tip of the iceberg for Michele and Tony. There was more to deal with.

Just prior to the discovery of the cancer, Tony had taken a leave of absence from his job, so both Tony and Michele were concerned about how to pay for the aggressive treatment protocol doctors recommended at the prestigious Gibbs Cancer Center & Research Institute in Spartanburg, South Carolina. Fortunately, the Bearden-Josey Center for Breast Health, adjacent to the Gibbs Cancer Center & Research Institute, paid for the start of her treatments. Doctors wanted to start chemotherapy before the prescribed partial mastectomy, and they biopsied the tissue around the lump as well as Michele's lymph nodes. They also recommended radiation five days a week for six weeks.

As with many women, Michele's cancer was estrogen receptor-positive (ER-positive). ER-positive breast cancer is the most common type of breast cancer diagnosed today. According to the American Cancer Society, about two out of every three cases of breast cancer are hormone receptor-positive. Most of these cases are ER-positive, meaning that there are estrogen receptors on the surface of the cancer cells that bind to estrogen. As a result, Michele was prescribed hormone therapy to block the estrogen.

What Michele hadn't expected was the immediate impact of the hormone therapy regimen.

"It launched me into immediate menopause," Michele said. "That was really tough to deal with at first."

Michele will remain on the hormone therapy for 10 years.

Throughout it all, Michele's strong faith sustained her—along with the incredible support she received.

"My church family cooked meals and helped me care for our children, which was even more critical due to the 'chemo brain' I experienced," Michele said.

Cancer survivors often use the term "chemo brain" to describe problems with thinking and memory that can occur after cancer treatment. Chemo brain is also known as chemo fog, chemotherapy-related cognitive impairment, or cognitive dysfunction.

Michele credits two other special people in her life with sustaining her throughout her treatment.

"Tony and my sister-in-law were with me every step of the way. I couldn't have done it without them."

During this time, Michele found that she couldn't use most brands of deodorant and body lotion. She was excited to discover Lemongrass Spa products.

"I wholeheartedly believe in the mission of Lemongrass Spa,"

Michele said. "I love Lemongrass Spa products because they are so natural. We're the only ones who have control over what we put into and on our bodies."

Michele's experience is still quite recent, and she knows there may be more twists and turns in the road. As she continues her journey, she is absolutely confident in the sustenance she receives from the faith that has always guided her life.

Finding Unexpected Strength

In the fall of 2004, Norah Anne Graham, 61, a university librarian in Toronto, Ontario, Canada, began experiencing bouts of vomiting. It was a very stressful time. Her beloved mother was seriously ill. Norah Anne, who was in her late forties at the time, believed the nausea was a menopausal symptom. With so much going on in her personal life, she didn't approach her physician with her concerns.

"I was simply too busy and too overwhelmed," Norah Anne said. "Quite frankly, I figured it would all just go away in time."

But it didn't go away.

In fact, it got worse.

Norah Anne's mother died in early December. Soon after, the vomiting started to come with abdominal pain. Even in the midst of her severe emotional distress, this concerning new development persuaded Norah Anne to make an appointment with her family physician.

Norah Anne's doctor understood right away that her situation was not typical of menopause. He immediately ordered a pelvic ultrasound.

When the doctor himself called Norah Anne the day after the ultrasound, she knew it wasn't a good sign.

"I wanted to believe I'd be okay," Norah Anne said. "But an inner voice told me I wasn't."

The doctor next referred Norah Anne to a nearby gynecologic oncologist, who recommended a full hysterectomy—removal of her cervix, uterus, and Fallopian tubes.

The surgeon Norah Anne saw next said that he couldn't be sure about the tumor's potential malignancy until it was removed. But he didn't seem very optimistic. And with good reason: The growth inside Norah Anne's pelvis and abdomen was the size of a bread box.

"I knew I had had major bloating and weight gain leading up to the surgery," Norah Anne recalls. "But I had assumed it was menopause again."

Norah Anne emerged from anesthesia and had her answer about the tumor right away. Her cousin had accompanied her to the operation. Norah Anne could tell from the expression on her face that what they had feared was indeed true.

The surgeon sent her back to the oncologist, who then outlined a course of eight weeks of weekly chemotherapy treatments.

As Norah Anne contemplated the journey she was about to begin, she thought about how she would cope.

"The weeks and months leading up to the diagnosis had been so incredibly tough," Norah Anne remembered. "Normally, I knew I would have collapsed from the strain following my mom's passing. But now that wasn't possible."

As a single woman with no siblings, Norah Anne also wondered how she would get to her appointments, especially because she worried about feeling ill on the drive home. Fortunately, two long-time family friends were available. One friend volunteered to drive her to

> *Heal me, Lord, and I will be healed; save me and I will be saved, for you are the one I praise.*
>
> —JEREMIAH 17:14

and from the appointments, and the other friend, a former nurse, offered to come with her to every appointment. This proved to be invaluable during those times when her medical team was providing details about the treatment protocol and Norah Anne found it difficult to focus on what they were saying.

As the chemotherapy treatments wore on, Norah Anne had to summon inner strength she didn't know she had.

"There were times I just lay on the couch crying, wondering how I could possibly go to the next day's appointment," Norah Anne said. "I thought about my father, who was a wonderful man who at times could become very discouraged by adversity, and I thought about my mother, who had fought her own battle against cancer more than 20 years earlier. I knew that both of them wouldn't want me to give up.

"I also learned what a difference laughter makes," Norah Anne said. "Watching *The Simpsons*—Bart Simpson in particular—got me through many dark moments."

After a long spring of treatments, Norah Anne's chemotherapy ended in April. Along with her cousin, she celebrated with a visit to the United States, visiting her other cousin, who had just given birth. Then Norah Anne booked a joyous trip to St. Kitts, where she put her feet in the warm water, basked in the Caribbean sunlight, and contemplated the sources of strength that had surrounded her in the preceding months.

"My friends and family were incredible," Norah Anne said. "I couldn't have gotten through it without them. As I look back, I know that I also couldn't have gotten through without reaching deep down inside myself. Fighting cancer proved to me that in adversity, unexpected strength can be found."

Norah Anne currently has a number of other chronic health challenges, including diabetes and kidney disease. She credits her fight with cancer with giving her the perseverance needed to endure.

"You can never know what you are capable of—until you have no choice but to find out," Norah Anne observed. "I draw on this experience for every challenge in my life."

Feeling Grateful Despite Her Challenges

Lauri Ricker, 52, a mom of six children and the wife of a minister, relies on devotional readings and the Bible for guidance and positivity in her life.

"My faith has always been so very important to me," Lauri said.

After Lauri was diagnosed with and treated for breast cancer, her faith became even more important. Lauri's faith—along with the support of her family and friends—was key in helping her get through one of the most difficult times in her life.

Lauri, who lives in Hagerstown, Maryland, had gotten false positive mammograms in the past. This made her diligent about doing breast self-exams. Also, she routinely went to a breast surgeon for a full evaluation after getting her regular mammograms.

In early 2016, Lauri's routine 3-D mammogram went smoothly. It showed no signs of cancer at all. But at Lauri's follow-up appointment with her breast surgeon, he found a swelling in her lymph nodes in the back of her armpit. An ultrasound suggested that it was just a cyst, but when the cyst was aspirated it was discovered that it was not a cyst, but an enlarged lymph node. Because it was under her arm, it was missed during Lauri's self-exam, a recent exam by her ob-gyn, and even by her mammogram.

In the spring of that year, Lauri had surgery to remove 15 lymph nodes. She learned that nine of them were cancerous. Consequently, Lauri's oncologist prescribed 20 sessions of chemotherapy and 25 treatments of radiation.

On Lauri's first day of chemo, she met a woman who had been getting chemo treatments for a while.

"You're going to make it through," the woman told Lauri.

Lauri held on to those words for dear life.

"There were days when I would think, 'I can't do this,'" she said.

By a little bit of serendipity, Lauri's path crossed with that woman again on the woman's last day of chemo. Lauri thanked her for her words.

"We connected on a deep spiritual, emotional level," Lauri said. "We were both going through the same thing."

As the chemo treatments went on, they made Lauri nauseated and exhausted.

"I felt a tiredness that was so severe I can't really even explain it," she said.

When that severe exhaustion hit, Lauri literally had to sit down, wherever she was. She couldn't do anything else. Before undergoing cancer treatment, Lauri was never one to take naps. But during treatment, she began taking daytime naps as a way to rejuvenate.

The chemo also came with physical side effects. She lost her hair, and she had to deal with painful mouth sores.

"When you lose your eyelashes and eyebrows, that's when you really look sick," Lauri said.

Keeping the Faith in God—and Medicine

Lauri started to wear a wig or headscarf.

The chemo and its side effects also took a toll on Lauri emotionally. She leaned heavily on her husband, sister, and a couple of good friends. During those times, she appreciated hearing "I love you" and comments such as, "Your coloring looks good today."

Because Lauri was so tired during treatment, she had to give up doing a lot of the things she used to love. But she found new appreciation for the things that she *could* do. For example, Lauri and her husband have six children in their blended family, ranging in age from 19 to 42. Every year, the younger three kids accompany Lauri and her husband to the beach in North Carolina. At first, Lauri's doctor told her that she shouldn't make the trip. Later, he relented and said that she *could* go if she promised to stay out of the sun because her cancer treatment made it easier for her skin to burn.

Instead of feeling sorry for herself while the rest of the family was at the beach during the day, Lauri found joy in cooking dinner and watching movies with her family later. At night, after the sun went down, she took walks on the beach and picked up shells.

Along the same lines, before Lauri's diagnosis, she loved participating in church missions, volunteering, and gardening. She became a master gardener, and prior to her diagnosis, she taught children how to grow flowers, fruits, and vegetables.

During treatment, Lauri couldn't volunteer or garden. So her husband took her to a garden center, where she chose the plants she wanted, and her family planted them for her. Instead of taking her usual walks, Lauri bought canvases and painted pictures of flowers and trees.

Today, Lauri is cancer-free. She has finished all her therapies, and her hair is growing back. In some ways, her life isn't much different from before she was diagnosed with cancer.

"The daily activities you do as a wife and mom are still the same post-cancer," Lauri said. But the difference? Lauri says that now she takes more joy in daily life.

"If I want to go to lunch with a friend, I go to lunch," she said. "I used to say, 'No, I can't do that today.'"

Lauri also finds that she and her husband are closer now. They talk more, they plan activities, and they *follow through* with the activities.

"We have an intent behind our lives now that we didn't have before," she said.

Lauri also takes more time for devotional and Bible reading, and she takes time to meditate and think about what she's grateful for. Some days that might be as simple as a good dinner she had or a phone call with a friend. Other days, it's as grand as living the joy-filled life that she still leads.

"My meditation helps me feel more positive," Lauri said. "God got me through a very rough time."

Sometimes, God was the only one Lauri could cry out to, and she did. On some especially dark days, Lauri asked God for a sign that she would get through her cancer treatment. A sign always came: The sun would shine brighter, a dear friend would call, or a basket of flowers would arrive.

Lauri couldn't go to church or help with Bible school during her treatment because she was told not to be around crowds due to the weakening effect chemo had on her immune system. Now, Lauri again attends church and finds strength from the communion service.

"Cancer makes you very aware of the spiritual things you want to be involved in," she said. "I'm so grateful to be able to do those things."

Summoning the Angels— and a Vacuum Cleaner

One evening in 2016, Amy Musser, a 43-year-old spiritual advisor in Hellertown, Pennsylvania, was watching a movie with her boyfriend. She stood up—and almost blacked out.

"I got up to go to the bathroom, but I could hardly walk," Amy remembered.

Gravely concerned, Amy's boyfriend called 911, and the paramedics rushed her to the nearest hospital.

At the hospital, they tested Amy's blood and urine. The emergency physicians discovered that her potassium was low, so they administered potassium intravenously and sent her home.

Little did they know, low potassium was the least of Amy's problems.

"My gut was telling me that there was more to it than that," she said. "Much more."

The emergency physician had told Amy to see her family physician if she didn't feel better, so Amy called her doctor the next day.

At that visit, Amy's family physician asked her to stand with her eyes closed. She started to fall over backward! The doctor had quick reflexes, and he caught her before she hit the floor.

Without hesitation, the family physician sent Amy back to the emergency department for a CT scan of her brain and to check her potassium levels again.

A few minutes later, the emergency physician gave Amy the news.

"You have a mass on your brain," the doctor said.

"I was completely shocked," Amy said. "My health had been perfect. I hadn't been to see a doctor in a very long time. I almost *never* took any medication. I went to the gym three to five times a week, and I was a runner. I didn't have any symptoms—no headaches, dizziness, or fatigue."

The diagnosis was even more shocking because Amy had been making great efforts to live a very healthy lifestyle.

"I had been slowly changing to using all-natural cosmetics and toiletries, which I was surprised to find cost less and last longer than many conventionally made products," Amy said. "I also started eating more organic food—although with a teenager in the house, it's too expensive to eat *all* organic! My son will eat a carton of organic strawberries in one sitting."

As a medium, Amy said that the angels had urged her to make these changes. "They want us to lead a cleaner life," she said.

Amy was admitted to the hospital right away. An MRI (magnetic resonance imaging) scan of her brain revealed an almond-size mass resting on her frontal lobe. It was a grade 3 anaplastic astrocytoma, which is a very rare type of brain tumor, especially in adults.

The doctors put Amy on steroids and anti-seizure medicine to keep Amy's brain from swelling and to prevent seizures. They sent her home for two weeks to give the medications a chance to work, and then she returned for surgery.

"Some days there won't be a song in your heart. Sing anyway"

—EMORY AUSTIN

"The surgery itself was a piece of cake," Amy said. "They didn't even have to shave my head. My daughter has her head half shaved, and she wanted me to shave my head so I would look like her."

After the surgery, Amy needed both chemotherapy and radiation. Once all of that medicine kicked in, Amy's symptoms began.

"It felt like there was too much going on in front of my face," she described. "I was bothered by loud noises and too much action. I even had to wear earplugs at my son's football games.

"The steroids made me gain 30 pounds in four weeks," Amy added. "The medicine made me moody and sleepy. I had felt better when I was recovering from the surgery than I did on all of that medicine."

With a long road of treatments ahead, Amy knew she needed to do something different to make it through. "I vowed I was going to heal myself," she said.

Amy's positivity switched on right away. "My dad has always said, 'It's 10 percent what happens to you, and 90 percent how you deal with it.' I focused very much on that."

So Amy did something not many people would think of to do: She called in the angels.

"I visualized my body surrounded in green light. Green is the color of healing; think of all of the green outside in nature," Amy said. "Every day, I would pray and call the angels in, saying, 'Please let me know I'm on the right path.' In particular, I called the angel of healing—Archangel Raphael—out loud or in my head."

Even with such a positive attitude, the chemo pills were very hard to swallow. Amy had to take them before every radiation treatment. Being so staunchly opposed to taking medicine, and knowing that chemo has huge potential to cause side effects, Amy found it hard to make herself take it.

"Every time I tried to take the chemo pills, I'd cry and gag because I didn't want to put them in my body," Amy said. "I knew that I had to change my thinking. So when I took the pills, I would say to my cells, 'All right, guys, this is for your highest good. This is for healing.' I never say *kill* or *battle* cancer; I always say *heal*."

Amy's doctor had warned her that the chemo would cause nausea—not could, but *would*. She even prescribed anti-nausea medication. Amy didn't want to take it.

"I visualized healing, green light in my stomach. I breathed in healing green light, and I exhaled gray light—representing negative emotions," Amy said. "I would ask my angels, 'Let me take this medicine without having any side effects.'"

Amy was then able to take the chemo pills without feeling any negative side effects at all. She didn't even have to take the anti-nausea medication.

Amy used visualization during her radiation treatments as well, to help her make it through. When she walked into the waiting room for her first radiation treatment, it felt like everyone sitting in that room was dying.

"I thought to myself, *I am not going to be like these people*," Amy said. She meditated on it. She visualized Archangel Michael using a vacuum cleaner to suck all of the negative energy out of the room.

"Within a few days, the energy of that room had changed," she said.

Amy's visualization didn't end in the waiting room, however.

> *"Being deeply loved by someone gives you strength, while loving someone deeply gives you courage."*
>
> —LAO TZU

"While I was receiving the 10 to 15 minutes of radiation, I kept thinking to myself, *This is going to work*," Amy said. "I would lie there and visualize Jesus's hands on my head. He's the master healer, after all! I visualized the color green and flowers blooming in my head, with fairies watering them and angels jumping around and singing 'Joy to the World'! I also imagined green blankets around the tumor. A friend of mine suggested I imagine giving my cancer cells hot tea and chicken noodle soup.

"It was amazing," Amy continued. "The more I did this, the more angels I saw circling around me in the radiation room."

Another technique Amy used is affirmation. When she had a worried thought or wavering faith, she said to herself, "I'm the loving operator of my mind."

Because Amy had gained so much weight, she didn't like looking at herself in the mirror. She wrote affirmations on Post-it notes and stuck them all over her mirror.

"Now I see the affirmations instead of myself!" Amy said. "Those words have kept me grounded and focused on moving forward."

Each night before bed, Amy tries to meditate. This helps her to relax and also to call upon her body's healing abilities. She found many free healing meditations on YouTube.

Despite aggressive treatment, Amy knows that the type of tumor she had has a 99 percent chance of coming back. She takes heart in a joke one of her friends made, "You've never been normal, so why start now?"

"I don't want to be a statistic," Amy asserted. "I know that our bodies can heal themselves. Think of the last time you had a cut on your finger. Did it heal? Of course!"

Praying for a Cure

In 1986, Brent Camden, then 41 was hospitalized with a bleeding stomach ulcer. The doctors fought to staunch the bleeding. He required 13 units of blood.

Brent quickly got back to his life as a civil engineer. Life went on.

Then in October 2014, Brent started to have stomach pains at night. His doctor recommended Prilosec-type medications, which helped. For a while.

In September 2015, the stomach pain came back with a vengeance. Brent's doctor ordered an endoscopy to examine his stomach. After the endoscopy on November 18, 2015, Brent was fully expecting and prepared to hear that another ulcer was the problem.

Unfortunately, Brent's doctor had other news.

"I was just coming out of the anesthesia," Brent said. "My doctor told me that I had about a five-inch-long tumor on my stomach wall that was probably cancer. That woke me up real quick."

Brent had to wait for a few days until the lab work came back for a definitive diagnosis. It turned out to be a large B-cell lymphoma.

Brent scheduled an oncology consultation for December 2nd. Before then, he had planned to take a Thanksgiving trip to Florida to meet up with some other family members.

"We decided to go ahead with the trip," Brent said. "I made the mistake of reading the tales about stomach cancer on the internet, many of which involved removal of the stomach and the lifestyle changes associated with that procedure. This greatly increased my anxiety for the next few days."

While Brent was driving home from Florida, his oncologist called. He put Brent's worries somewhat at ease. When Brent returned from the beach and met with him on December 2nd, to his relief the recommended treatment wasn't surgery, nor radiation. Instead, the doctor recommended a treatment called CHOP-R, which consists of five drugs—Cyclophosphamide, Vincristine, Rituximab, Doxorubicin, and Prednisone.

"I thought the acronym choice was unduly harsh!" Brent said. "What about CURE-R? That would have made me feel a whole lot better."

The doctor assured Brent that if you have to get cancer, this is the one to have.

"The cure rate for this type of cancer is around 90 percent," Brent's doctor told him confidently.

The first thing Brent had to do was stop taking the injections of Enbrel for his rheumatoid arthritis (RA).

"I was assured that the meds in the chemo would keep the RA in check during treatment," Brent said. "My RA had been so bad in the past that I could hardly get off the couch for the pain. The Enbrel had kept it in check, but as the ads on TV suggest, one of the side effects is possible lymphoma. The doctor suspected this was the

> "*God is the great physician. His specialty is heart transplants.*"
>
> —MARTIN TOMBACK

cause of my cancer, and I would probably have to give up the shot treatments."

The chemo would consist of six treatments, each 21 days apart. The first started on December 11th, and it was an eight-hour marathon.

"They started with blood work, and then I had to wait for those results," Brent said. "With those results, the doctor determined if I was healthy enough for the treatment and what the dose of each drug should be. Then we started the infusions in the vein, the longest of them took about four hours."

Brent quickly learned that the first five days after the infusion were the worst. Because his body was so weakened by the chemo, he had to take another medicine in high doses for these days.

"This functions almost like an upper to keep the body from sinking too low," Brent said. "The problem is, it made me so very hyper that I couldn't sleep much at night. I also experienced night chills and sweats. My whole body would shake for up to 15 minutes, and then I'd wake up later completely drenched in sweat."

After the first week, Brent's strength would gradually return—until the next infusion—but never quite back to normal. Each infusion gradually made Brent weaker.

"During this time, my wife and I were able to replace the wood on our deck, so there were many decent days," Brent said. "I was pleasantly surprised to have no nausea during the treatment. I was really dreading that part. Eating became a problem just because most food didn't taste good or the smell turned me off. The treatments continued until early March 2016. I had to be admitted to the hospital for a few days for dehydration once. It was difficult to drink as much fluid as needed because the drugs gave all fluids a metal taste. I also had to give up caffeine because it dehydrates the body."

About halfway through Brent's treatment, he had a CT scan on his stomach that showed the tumor had shrunk a lot. This boosted his morale significantly. He had the last treatment on April 4, 2016, and a PET (positron emission tomography) scan on May 11, 2016, showed no more cancer.

"The side effects of the drugs take up to a year to dissipate, so I am back to normal now (less about 20 pounds lost during the process). I met with my doctor in January 2017, and he said I had the blood work of a 20-year-old. I wish my joints knew that! Unless I start to have problems, I won't have any more scans or treatments," he reported.

The physical challenges were hard on Brent's body, but far less expected were the mental challenges.

"Being diagnosed at age 70 is much different than at a younger age," Brent said. "I felt like I had lived a full life, and I was ready to move on if it had worked out that way. I have a strong faith, but I felt that at some point, the faith must allow the doctors to come into the picture and do their thing. My cancer journey required both. The important part of the equation is to keep a positive outlook throughout the process."

One thing Brent found to help him combat both the physical and mental challenges was exercising.

"I tried to exercise whenever I could," Brent said. "It was tough at times because of the feeling of isolation. My doctors urged me to avoid large crowds because my immune system was so weak. This was tough in the winter because my wife and I like to walk in the mall or large stores."

Isolation can be a common challenge for people fighting cancer.

"I find that friends tend to be afraid to call," Brent said. "Probably they're afraid they will disturb you—so they get info some other way. This added to my feelings of isolation. I had a close friend die from a prolonged cancer a little earlier, and it was difficult for me to try to communicate with him when he was battling cancer."

Brent is grateful for his recovery and his health. Like many cancer survivors, he's quick to praise the physicians and hospital staff who helped him.

"My treatment was done at the VA hospital in Lexington, Kentucky," Brent said. "I couldn't have been happier with the treatment I received. The physicians, nurses, and staff were always there for me. The nurses in the infusion area see people who are in different stages, coping in different ways, and some still have issues related to their military service. They treat everyone with respect. Most of the time, they never find out whether or not the patient was cured—unless they return later for more treatments. It's a tough, thankless job, and my hat's off to those amazing folks.

"During my chemo treatments, I developed a split nail on one thumb," Brent said. "This is normally not a big deal, but the side effects of chemo (rashes, etc.) and the lack of adequate immunity at this time raise questions about potential infections. My daughter suggested that I try Lemongrass Spa's Organic Skin and Nail Balm. I started using this on the nail, and the problem completely cleared up in just a few weeks. This blessedly gave me one less thing to worry over during this stage, and it has not returned."

Today, Brent is about one month away from being cancer-free for a year.

> *"Attitude is a little thing that makes a big difference."*
>
> —WINSTON CHURCHILL

"I don't think you can ever say that you have beaten cancer," Brent said. "It's like being an alcoholic. Once a cancer victim, always a cancer victim. It was in your body and could return. I just thank God for the healing power of the medical treatments and pray for a total cure someday."

Trusting in God's Plan

In March 2011, Heather Miller, 43, had a great deal on her mind.

Heather recalls standing in her muggy garage in Camp Lejeune, North Carolina, watching her husband, Gordon, pack for an upcoming rapid deployment to Libya. A Marine Lieutenant Colonel and a member of the Corps since 1994, Gordon was serving as a Battalion Landing Team Commanding Officer of 1,300 marines and sailors living across three ships.

That day, Gordon asked Heather to hand him a piece of his gear.

"As I leaned against a Christmas bin to grab what he needed, I felt a strange sensation on my chest," Heather said. "I shrugged it off, overcome with the gravity of the situation that was at hand."

With good reason: This deployment was for an unknown length of time. Heather would be taking care of their six-year-old son, Ryan, by herself and actively supporting the more than 1,300 wives, girlfriends, and parents at the base through the deployment.

Soon, Heather began preparing for her parents' planned Easter visit. The day they were scheduled to arrive, she was taking a shower.

She remembered that it had been a few months since she had performed her last breast self-exam.

"I felt a lump," Heather said. "Immediately, I knew that something was wrong. In my heart, I knew it was cancer."

Heather asked her mom to check it as well.

"You had better get this checked," her mom said.

Heather quickly went to see her doctor, who scheduled a mammogram and a core biopsy.

Within a few days, she received a call from the doctor's office to come in right away.

A woman of strong faith, Heather believes in the Scripture verse, Philippians 4:19: "And my God will supply every need of yours according to his riches in glory in Christ Jesus."

Heather says that God provided her native New Yorker friend Joey, who lived a few doors down at the time. Joey accompanied Heather to the doctor's office where they were escorted to the exam room in short order. Soon, the doctor and Heather's son's pediatrician (both family friends) joined them.

The doctor struggled to get the words out. Through tears, she said, "It is not what we had hoped for, Heather. You have stage 2B breast cancer, and it is aggressive." Heather was 37.

As the news sank in, Heather was comforted by her three dear friends, all in tears while her husband was half a world away.

Yet for Heather, there were no tears. In fact, there were no *fears*.

"I wasn't shocked," Heather said. "I felt complete and perfect peace—peace that allowed me to focus on finding out details about the cancer and where I would go for treatment."

Heather knew that God surrounded her with exactly what she needed.

"I really believe that as a type A personality, I needed a room full of friends who loved me dearly but could not hold it together," Heather said. "This caused me to fall into the role that I do best: loving and caring for people. I'm the one my friends call when they need help. If you have a crisis, I'm your girl. God knew this, of course! He designed me and knows how I am wired. God gave me *His* peace to handle what I had just heard and reassure my dear friends too. But God was not done!"

Heather was immediately surrounded by a broader base of support.

"Word travels fast on a small military base," Heather said. "My home was quickly filled with women bringing plates of dinner, chocolate, and wine—but most of all their love and support. They rallied around me. My friends watched Ryan while I made phone calls, the hardest of which was to my husband. But still in perfect peace, I managed to convince my husband of a really great idea, which had come to me directly from God."

Heather determined that Gordon would not return to the United States right away.

"He had a job to do, and so did I," Heather said. "He would fight the bad guys, and I would fight cancer. Of course, he objected. He was ready to jump off the ship and swim the Atlantic to be by my side. Still, I had peace and calm; I knew that it would be okay. And I knew that this is what we were supposed to do. It took some time and some tears, but eventually Gordon agreed to my great idea."

As the sun began to set on a very long day, Heather explained to Ryan that she would be sick for a while and look different. Heather told her young son that she would lose her hair and be tired, but she explained that God would be with them through everything. Young Ryan did not fully understand.

"As I leaned down to kiss him good night, I saw complete and utter trust in his eyes," Heather said. "I witnessed the faith of a child, with trust in his mommy and in his Heavenly Father."

> *"Hope is being able to see that there is light despite all of the darkness."*
>
> —DESMOND TUTU

Still Heather felt some uncertainty and doubt that night.

"I shut off the lights in the hallway, walked into my room, gently closed the door, and crawled into bed," Heather said. "I cried out to my savior, 'Please heal me! Please show me your purpose for my life! Please allow me to see my son grow up, allow me to grow old with my husband, and allow me to care for my parents as they age!'"

After a while, Heather fell into a peaceful sleep. As the early morning light streamed into her bedroom, Heather realized she had experienced God's presence that night.

"In the sunlight beams that danced across the floor, He was present," Heather said. "God's presence filled me with hope. God's work in me was not done!"

Through Heather's treatment, she was blessed to have her parents by her side.

"No matter how old you are, you really want your mom when you're sick," Heather said. "I was not alone. God surrounded me with an army of earthly angels!"

Heather believes in many ways it was the best of times and the hardest of times. During this period, she endured a double mastectomy, 16 rounds of chemotherapy, 33 rounds of radiation treatments, an oophorectomy (removal of her ovaries), and a year of treatments. She also learned through her treatment that her breast cancer was not genetic but had environmental causes.

"There were parabens in my tumor, which mimicked estrogen in my body and were one of the main driving forces of my cancer," Heather said. "Because of this, I began searching for truly safe products."

Heather's devout faith manifested itself in those closest to her.

"Throughout my treatment, God delivered the same message," Heather said. "He chose many different people to tell me."

She said the most profound message came from her son, Ryan.

"A few weeks after I lost my hair to chemotherapy, I was sitting on the floor of my son's room," Heather said. "Ryan was playing with his LEGOs, and I was trying to tune into his little six-year-old heart. I wondered, *How was he really handling things?* I was asking him if he was worried or scared since Mommy lost her hair. He glanced up at me and said, 'No, Mommy' and went right back to playing. I told him, 'Okay, because you know this is only for a while. Mommy will get better, and there is no need to worry.'

"Then Ryan stopped playing with his LEGOs. His little hands grabbed my hands and held them tight. He looked me in the eye and said, 'Mommy, Jesus told me you will be fine. I am not worried.'

"Then he went right back to playing with his LEGOs. Wow! A message from Heaven! At that moment, I needed to have the faith of a child, like Ryan. I received this message, and it still continues to sustain me."

Heather's cancer experience was not easy, especially for her husband, who had the weight of the world on his shoulders.

"It was a lot for Gordon," Heather said. "He was thousands of miles away, in command during a tense time globally, with a wife who had cancer. I feared that Gordon might pull away or resent God. I prayed to God to allow this trial to draw Gordon closer to Him and to unite us in our faith. I prayed but didn't hear anything from God at first, but that was because God was busy! God was truly on the move, sowing seeds in Gordon that would grow his faith and draw him closer to Christ. God was not done with Gordon. He was surrounding him! He was present."

Heather is committed to her belief in the omnipresence of God. "God may close a door on you. Maybe it is something that you really wanted or what you thought He wanted for you. Trust Him. He has something greater planned." A Scripture verse, Jeremiah 29:11, describes it beautifully: "For I know the plans I have for you," declares the Lord, "plans to prosper you and not to harm you, plans to give you hope and a future."

It wouldn't be long until God revealed that purpose to Heather.

In March 2012, she was given the opportunity to be a national spokesperson for a breast cancer awareness organization.

"I would be on the talk show circuits, sharing my story, promoting this organization, and spreading awareness about breast cancer," Heather said. "I was really, really excited about this. I thought to myself, *This is what I am supposed to do with my healing*. But God had a different path already set for me. I felt this overwhelming desire to research this organization and learned that this organization supported other major companies who used chemicals in skin care products—and that they also funded other organizations that did not uphold biblical principles. I knew that God did not want me there, and I had to walk away because He shut the door. I was really disappointed. And I thought, *Well, God's work in me is done*. How silly that was. He is *never* done with us, and He is always with us and for us. I just let my disappointment overshadow *His* plan!"

Although that door was closed, it eventually led to Lemongrass Spa's lime green door. Now Heather is a senior director at Lemongrass Spa.

"I asked God, 'If this is where you want me, then please anoint and bless this path,'" Heather said. "Because of Lemongrass Spa, I am able to share my story and help educate others every single day. But I am not doing this alone, and it is not about me. Lemongrass Spa offers products that help and not harm—products that reduce the toxic burden and cancer risk for all."

Heather fully embraces her platform of bringing awareness and hope to people living with cancer.

"As leaders and as women, we spend a lot of time taking care of others," Heather said. "We often put ourselves last on the to-do list. However, to take care of others, we must first take care of ourselves. I encourage everyone I know to perform a monthly breast self-exam because they truly save lives, and I am living proof. That breast self-exam in 2011 saved my life, and as a result, I am now a five-year cancer survivor. There is a free app that you can download to your phone, and it will send you a monthly reminder to do your breast self-exam. It is called "Keep a Breast." Please download this free app and give yourself the gift of self-care."

Heather says, "I want to encourage everyone to trust that God is present and around you. Look for Him in the unexpected places. He is by your side in tears and in laughter, and He will equip you with what you need! He does have great plans for you, even though sometimes the path is hard. Lean into Him. Seek His voice to guide you down that path. Know that even in the hardest, darkest times, there is hope. The hope He has for you!"

Proverbs 3:5–6 perfectly captures Heather's approach to life: "Trust in the Lord with all your heart and lean not on your own understanding; in all your ways submit to Him, and He will make your paths straight."

She believes in it with all her heart. "God is not done with you. He has laid out a beautiful plan, a beautiful path, and a beautiful story for each one of you."

Part 4

CHOOSING A NATURAL, CHEMICAL-FREE LIFE

As most of us careen through our hurry-scurry lives, we rarely give much thought to the products we use every day to make our lives easier. What's in your toothpaste, body wash, hair spray? Which chemicals do you use to clean your countertops, oven, toilets? Do you spray products on your flowers to make them grow and on the weeds to make them *stop* growing? With what do you wash your car, porch, deck?

If you look at the ingredients lists—probably using a magnifying glass because they're in 4-point type to try to keep your attention off of them—what would you find? If you can't even pronounce an ingredient let alone know what it is, do you really want to put it on and in your body?

Your skin is your largest organ, and any product that comes into contact with your skin enters your body. Yet shampoos, lotions, and makeup can contain a number of toxins, such as parabens and phthalates, which have been identified as hormone disruptors and may be linked to certain cancers.

When shopping for cosmetics and personal-care products, read the ingredients labels. Avoid anything that includes the words "paraben" (often used as a suffix, as in methylparaben) or "phthalate" (listed as dibutyl and diethylhexyl or just "fragrance"). Or visit CosmeticsDatabase.com, a website created by the Environmental Working Group (EWG.org) that identifies the toxic ingredients of thousands of personal-care products.

Certainly, you're not putting household cleaning products on your skin, but it's really difficult to avoid breathing in their fumes and touching their sprays. Plus, many products leave residue on surfaces, so when you touch them later, the chemicals can still be absorbed into your skin.

There is no proven link between cancer and household products. But a variety of goods contain hormone disruptors, chemicals that can mimic or interfere with hormones, such as estrogen. Some researchers believe that these chemicals can cause normal cells to abnormally divide. Then each and every time the cells divide, there's the risk of mutation, which can lead to cancer.

A great deal of research has been conducted and more is being done to understand possible environmental influences on cancer risk. Compounds in the environment that have estrogen-like properties are of special interest. For example, substances and PCBs (polychlorinated biphenyls) found in some plastics, certain cosmetics and personal care products, and pesticides, seem to have such properties. In theory, these could affect cancer risk.

It's unlikely that you'll toss out all of your skin care products, makeup, and cleaners all at once. But it's important to choose the safest products possible for yourself and for your family.

You have the power to make better, healthier choices. Healthier choices can lead to a healthier you, a healthier family, and a healthier planet too!

Healing with Natural Products

Moving. The word induces stress and anxiety for all of those who have that listed in their plans. Military wives, however, have moved so many times, they almost have it down to a routine. But Patricia Myer's latest move was anything but routine.

Patricia, 41, a clinical social worker, had a checklist of things to do before her move. On the top of her list was her annual mammogram. Once that was accomplished, she felt like she could concentrate on packing up her home and moving her family 739 miles (as the crow flies) from Maryland to Alabama.

As Patricia was traveling to her new home in the South, she received an unexpected call from her doctor. Her mammogram was abnormal, and she needed a biopsy.

So Patricia went back to Maryland to get the necessary biopsy. The results of the biopsy showed she had stage one breast cancer. Knowing she didn't want to continue to travel back and forth, she made the decision to have her partial mastectomy in her new home state of Alabama. The results of a second biopsy during the surgery

> *"The art of healing comes from nature,
> not from the physician.
> Therefore the physician must start from
> nature, with an open mind."*
>
> —PARACELSUS

changed her diagnosis to triple negative one breast cancer. A biopsy of her lymph nodes brought good news that it had not spread to her lymph nodes.

Patricia sought out three different opinions. Fortunately, the three physicians' opinions were unanimous. *Unfortunately*, they all agreed that she should receive chemotherapy.

Patricia's four rounds of chemo started in June and ended in October. One of the worst side effects of her chemo was a leaking that resulted in red blisters, similar to a chemical burn, on her skin. Her doctors said it would take months for her skin to heal. But they didn't know about Healing Elements Balm from Lemongrass Spa.

Patricia tried the Healing Elements Balm on her skin.

"My blisters up cleared within a week!" Patricia said.

Even her doctors were surprised.

In November, Patricia had a month of radiation. The nurses recommend that their patients use creams such as vitamin E during treatments for their skin, but Patricia told them about her amazing experience with Healing Elements Balm, and she continued to use the product with great results.

Not surprisingly, Patricia is a huge fan of Healing Elements.

"It's the only thing that has helped my son's eczema," Patricia said.

Lemongrass Spa products have worked so well for Patricia that she's signing up to become a Lemongrass Spa consultant. While she looks forward to trying all of the Lemongrass products, she's really excited about switching from her makeup brand to Lemongrass Spa makeup.

In addition to the changes Patricia made to her beauty and skin care routines, she also made some changes to her diet. She eliminated "land meats" from her diet. Today, she gets her protein from eggs and fish. Patricia rarely eats gluten, and she works hard to live holistically.

Patricia, who's also a mother of a 16-year-old daughter and an eight-year-old son, is now in the maintenance phase of her cancer. She's already planning their next move—which will take them all the way to Germany.

"Surely, this move will be much less stress inducing than the last," Patricia said.

Changing-for the Better

After 20 years of being an Army wife, Ramona Mayo and her husband moved to Kentucky. They were enjoying the life of empty nesters—and all of the freedoms that come with it.

Breast cancer ran in Ramona's family, so she knew how important it was to get her yearly mammogram. But in 2010, for some reason, she put it off. Finally, though it was past due, she made it in to her annual appointment.

Ramona and her husband were on their way to Missouri to visit their daughter and granddaughter when her doctor called saying they needed her to come in for an ultrasound of her breast. Ramona told her doctor that she'd get the ultrasound done when she returned from her trip. The doctor didn't like that response. She stressed how important it was that Ramona come in right away.

Still, Ramona resisted.

True to her word, though, as soon as Ramona returned to Kentucky, she got the ultrasound. Following the ultrasound, she was told that she needed a biopsy. The biopsy revealed that Ramona had

> *"We cannot direct the wind,
> but we can adjust the sails."*
>
> —ANONYMOUS

cancer in her left breast. Ramona's radiologist insisted she also have a magnetic resonance imaging (MRI) scan, which Ramona felt was being overly aggressive.

It turned out to be the right move.

The results of that MRI confirmed that Ramona also had a small lesion in her right breast. She was diagnosed with bilateral breast cancer.

Physically, Ramona had felt fine. "If it weren't for those tests, I would have had no idea that I was sick," she said.

In April, when Ramona got the initial diagnosis, she was scared.

"I cried a lot," she confided.

Breast cancer is very prevalent in her family. Most of Ramona's family members, unfortunately, were not survivors.

In the beginning, Ramona spent a lot of time crying, praying, and going over the "what ifs."

"I started to journal, to express my feelings," Ramona said. "I came to the realization that if I gave it over to God, I might still be frightened, but at least I would have peace."

Friends, their church family, coworkers, and neighbors couldn't have been more supportive of Ramona during her treatment. In June, when Ramona had her bilateral mastectomy, chemotherapy, and radiation, Ramona's mother drove from Massachusetts to help. Friends visited with her and prayed for her. People stopped by with food and friendship.

"I was so incredibly touched by everyone's thoughtfulness,"

Ramona said. "I was especially grateful for my friends from all over the country who sent me hats—mostly hand knitted. I was almost overwhelmed by their support."

After Ramona's diagnosis, she tried to make changes to her diet.

"Change is hard!" Ramona said. "I'd make a change. A little while later, I'd get comfortable and slip back to my old habits. Then I'd regroup and try to eat healthy again."

In addition to changing what Ramona was putting *into* her body, she also changed what she put *onto* her body. She stopped dyeing her hair, and she switched to a natural deodorant.

One of Ramona's coworkers sells Lemongrass Spa products. When Ramona explained to her that she was trying to use fewer products with harmful chemicals, her coworker told her more about the company.

"She said that Lemongrass Spa products are good for you, and they also work really well," Ramona said.

Ramona's favorite Lemongrass Spa product is the Healing Elements Balm. She uses it for several things. She has found that it helped when she had to put on the compression sleeves for her lymphedema, which caused swelling in her arms. It also helped diminish her mastectomy scars. She also uses it as a deodorant in cooler weather.

"I buy Healing Elements tubes and gift them to friends and family. My granddaughter insists on using it whenever she has an itch."

Today, Ramona, 52, feels fantastic and is doing well. She's grateful that her doctors aggressively stay on top of everything. She's working as a secretary and enjoys her two grown children and two grandchildren.

But Ramona's no longer an empty nester. Now Ramona and her husband are raising their granddaughter in Rineyville, Kentucky. Life, again, has changed for the better.

Arming Herself with Information

When you ask most cancer survivors what their life was like pre-cancer diagnosis, they will say that life *pre*-cancer was dramatically different than their life *post*-cancer. The defining moment? The moment you found out you have cancer. Finding out that you have cancer changes everything.

Stay-at-home mom Frederica Christ of Pasco, Washington, had already had this life-shattering change before her own diagnosis. First, she had to walk through it with her husband.

In 2016, Fredrica's husband, Josef, was diagnosed with non-Hodgkin's lymphoma. Suddenly, Frederica became all too familiar with cancer. Her husband needed to have many rounds of intensive chemotherapy. Naturally, Frederica felt the urgency to jump into action and help him in every way she could. Her main focus at that time became supporting her husband. She wanted to be certain he received the care he needed. For a long time that was her main goal.

Frederica knew that an important part of supporting her husband to get healthy was doing her best to minimize the stress in their lives.

That is a huge undertaking in any circumstance, and Frederica did what she was able to keep things running smoothly. It was important that her husband be able to focus on recuperating and getting healthy.

And then in November of that same year, Frederica recalls that she felt a lump.

"I remember thinking to myself, *Oh bummer, I'm just gonna ignore this*," Frederica said.

That thought stayed with her for a while.

For a few months, Frederica did exactly what she told herself she would do. She ignored the lump. Life was hectic and busy. She and her husband had a 13-year-old daughter at home and three adult children as well. Then she and her husband decided to sell their house to downsize and make life simpler.

Finally, in January, Frederica stopped putting off seeking medical attention. She made an appointment to see her doctor. That's when Frederica learned that she had triple negative breast cancer in one lymph node.

"I decided to 'buck the system,'" Frederica said. "I wasn't going to just blindly follow what the doctors said."

Frederica started doing research. Lots of research.

"The more I learned, the more I thought to myself, *If I'm going to die, I don't want to die under chemo. I wanna be as much as me as possible*," Frederica said.

She also knew that she did not want radiation.

"These might not be the choices that other people would make, but I knew that they were the right choices for *me*," Frederica said.

She had the tumor removed.

Life had been full of changes for a while for Frederica and her husband with his health issues and then hers. So Frederica started to

> *"The best way to detoxify is to stop putting toxic things into the body and depend upon its own mechanism."*
>
> —ANDREW WEIL, MD

make her own changes as well—changes to support a healthier lifestyle.

First, Frederica changed her diet. She began testing her urine and saliva for pH conductivity and ureas. And she wasn't sleeping well. So she worked on changing that too.

"My husband was so very helpful and supportive," Frederica said. "He let me do my research, and he encouraged me to sleep when I could."

Frederica's research led her to make some changes in the foods that she put *in* her body—as well as the skin care products she used *on* her body. She wanted to expose her body to as few toxins as possible.

"Early on, I stopped using commercial deodorants," Frederica said. "I started to use Lemongrass Spa products because they seemed to be dedicated to healthy body care."

Frederica appreciates getting things that are as clean—free of additives, chemicals, and toxins— as possible.

"This takes time and research," Frederica said. "But I'm willing to do whatever it takes to live the way that I feel is healthiest."

If you ask Frederica where she found support with all that has been going on in her life, she'll tell you, "Mostly in God. My family big time, and specific friends."

But she was honest in saying that there are some friends who actually can't handle it.

"They weren't able to deal with me having cancer," Frederica said.

So she chooses not to focus on that. Instead, Frederica explains that you find the friends who *are* able to handle it and talk to them. Frederica adds that there are some things you may want to tell your friends that you don't want to tell your family.

Today, Frederica is happy—and hopeful.

"I'm good," Frederica said. "I am tired though, and that has driven me toward prayer and assessing what is truly important in life."

Today, Frederica is trying to be more patient. But she's doing the things that she wants to do.

"We had a reservation to go to Paris," Frederica said. "And so we went."

Choosing Safer Skin Care Products

Before Katie Bell's breast cancer diagnosis in 2016, she was a busy full-time mom, wife, and dedicated speech pathologist. She loved being active with her two boys, Carter, 11, and Liam, 9, and her husband, Joe.

Katie and Joe enjoyed running and biking together and watching their boys excel in sports. Downtime for the family was always appreciated at their cottage in Manistee Beach, Michigan.

Katie described her experience pre-cancer as, "living a perfect dream life."

She loved to be social and plan events with her friends and family. Her friends teased her about always being the one to organize the next "fun event." Concerts, barbeques, camping, bonfires, and Tiger's games, Katie loved being part of all these activities and more.

Life for Katie had a great work/play balance, and she was as diligent about her and her family's healthcare as she was about all of the other aspects of her life. So when Katie turned 40, getting her first mammogram was immediately on her list of things to do.

Little did Katie know, but that mammo was going to shatter her perfect dream life.

Katie's journey didn't end after her first mammogram. That turned into a second 3D mammogram, biopsy, partial mastectomy, and finally, a breast cancer diagnosis: ductal carcinoma in situ, grade 3.

When Katie's doctor called her with the news, she was optimistic about her treatment. The doctor explained that the type of cancer Katie had has a 97 percent cure rate, and it was non-invasive.

But still, hearing the diagnosis "cancer," no matter how curable, still packs an emotional wallop on a person. Cancer stops your life—like you've run smack into a brick wall. Life comes to a screeching halt.

"When my doctor called, there was a moment of silence, followed by tears, and then more silence as my mind processed the devastating information," Katie said.

Suddenly, Katie's life was filled with doctor's visits, hospital stays, a mastectomy, cancer treatments, and reconstructive surgeries.

Katie was surrounded by many friends and family members during her journey with cancer. Friends and family brought meals over, took her out on lunch dates, and kept in touch by sending countless cards.

"But still I felt lonely at times," Katie said. "Ultimately, your journey with cancer is one you have to walk alone."

Everyone's experience with the disease is different, and everyone needs to process it emotionally in their own way. Sometimes people can't help but feel alone.

In a beautifully written Facebook post, Katie talked about processing some of the many emotions, including the feelings of isolation. In another post, she said goodbye to her breast:

"Goodbye, my friend," Katie wrote. "You did your job. You nursed

"Scars are tattoos with better stories."

—ANONYMOUS

my beautiful babies, giving them what they needed to become the smart, healthy, strong, and amazing boys they are today. Guess what?! You *don't* define me as a woman or make me beautiful. Lately, you *do* remind me to make every day count and that I *am* a fighter, stronger than I ever knew, and that I'm in love with my life.

"Now, for some reason you're slowly poisoning my body. Why? I'll never know.

"Our 40-year journey together ends very soon. So, buh-bye, and take cancer with you."

This post shows Katie pulling from her inner strength to make her peace with cancer. It's something that is a personal journey and one that has to be made alone. We need the support of friends and family for everyday support, but it is ultimately up to the patient to make their peace with the disease as Katie has done so eloquently in her Facebook post and cancer journey.

Most oncologists would agree a positive attitude is essential to recovering from cancer.

Along with a new sense of inner strength, Katie's battle with cancer inspired her to change her lifestyle. She always embraced a balance of healthy eating, exercise, sleep, and wearing sunscreen, but after her diagnosis she became even more vigilant. She goes organic for the "dirty dozen," which is the Environmental Working Group's list of produce with the highest loads of pesticide residues. (For more information on the dirty dozen, go to EWG.org.)

Katie also goes organic with meats and diary, and she buys only non-GMO grains.

Many people don't think about it, but personal care products are also extremely likely to contain harmful chemicals. Katie uses the "Think Dirty" app to identify and then purchase beauty products without harmful carcinogens. The skin is our largest organ, and using natural products helps lower our exposure to harmful chemicals.

"I love Lemongrass Spa products," Katie said. "I especially love their Healing Elements Balm, which I've used on all my new "battle wounds" (scars), Ultra Hydrating Crème, body washes, and sugar scrubs. My good friend and sorority sister, Rachel, turned me onto these products before I was diagnosed. As I underwent treatments, she has continuously sent me products to try."

On Election Day November 2016, Katie got the news that her cancer was gone. Emotionally she has never felt stronger; however, physically her body is still recovering. She took time on this joyous day to take an emotional inventory.

"I realized that slowing down wasn't a bad thing," Katie said. "I feel that each small step that I take forward makes me physically and emotionally stronger."

Katie continues to give back to the cancer struggle by walking in the annual Susan J. Komen three-day events. Developing awareness about breast cancer through this organization and others is a priority in her life.

"Cancer is an emotional roller coaster," Katie said. "I felt loss, isolation, anger, and depression. But I also found strength, appreciation, growth, and empowerment."

Helping Others Choose Healthier Products

Donna Ellis, now 45, was living the dream in Kent, Washington. She was a happily married mother of three kids. Two of them were still living at home, and one was married and out of the house.

Donna loved her job working in the office at her kids' elementary school. She enjoyed exercising—especially running. She never got sick.

Even though Donna was grateful for all of the blessings in her life, she still had the nagging feeling that her life wouldn't *always* be this idyllic.

Like most busy moms, Donna was so consumed with taking care of everyone else that she put herself on the back burner. She knew that she should get her routine mammogram, but she kept putting it off because she couldn't find the time.

Days turned into weeks.

Weeks turned into months.

Before Donna knew it, an entire *year* had passed from the time she

> ## "Faith in God includes faith in His timing."
>
> —ANONYMOUS

should have gotten her routine exam. Summer vacation started in June. The school was closed. Donna was out of excuses.

"Finally, I had the time to get to the appointment that I had put off for so long," Donna said.

A couple of weeks after Donna finally had her mammogram, her doctor called to say they needed to check her again. Because this wasn't the first time Donna needed a second mammogram, she wasn't concerned. The second mammogram in July indicated that she needed an ultrasound on her left breast, which was performed right away.

The ultrasound revealed that Donna had several tumors, one of which was a starburst shape. With this finding, Donna knew that this was not going to have the results she had in the past.

"I knew that my idyllic life had come to a halt," Donna said. "I really didn't want to be right. But I was."

Several days after the ultrasound, Donna had a biopsy. Before the doctor called with the results, Donna had a meeting with a nurse to go over her care plan. She was able to go online to view her charts so it wasn't a total surprise when the doctor said that her test was positive for cancer.

"God put a timeline to make things happen when they did," Donna said. "I believe that's why we caught it when we did. I'm so grateful that my cancer was caught at stage one when it was small and slow growing."

Donna is also grateful that she didn't put her mammogram off any longer because her cancer likely would have progressed. She had never felt ill, and the lump was too small to feel.

Now Donna started to worry that something *else* might be wrong with her. But each time Donna met with her doctors, and the more they figured out how to treat her, the better she felt.

When Donna first found out she had cancer, she immediately thought she would have to undergo chemotherapy. She thought everyone with cancer was treated with chemo and/or radiation. That was not the case. Donna found out that no two cancers are alike, and each is treated according to its specific characteristics. She did have a mastectomy and found an amazing plastic surgeon for her reconstruction surgery. She will also take the medication tamoxifen for at least five years.

Donna felt a new desire for her body to be as strong as possible and to combat side effects of her medicine. So she sees a naturopath. So far, she has not experienced any side effects from her medication. Now she only needs to see her oncologist every six months. But she is more attuned to her body's aches and pains if something doesn't feel right.

"I really believe that I'll be fine, but I think it's human nature to be concerned," Donna said.

Everything has gone smoothly so far. While Donna wonders why she got cancer, she also feels blessed and that many prayers have been answered.

Only two weeks after her diagnosis, Donna attended a Lemongrass Spa party. The consultant at the party, Donna Parkhurst, explained that her mother's cancer diagnosis was the reason she started using and selling Lemongrass Spa products. Donna Ellis placed an order the night of the party. When she ordered the second time, she won the mystery hostess prize, and she received many different creams.

While she loved all the creams, Donna said that Healing Elements Balm was her favorite. She also loved the Ultra Hydrating Crème because it really soothed her skin without feeling greasy.

After Donna's second reconstruction surgery, she decided to do an experiment with her scar. She put Healing Elements Balm on half of the scar, and she put Body Butter by Lemongrass Spa on the other half. After several weeks, Donna determined that Healing Elements was best for healing the scar, while the Body Butter was best for fading the scar.

Today, Donna's exercising again. Her life is getting back to normal. She's grateful that she only missed two weeks of work.

And now she has a new job! Donna's experience with Lemongrass Spa products was so impressive that she became a consultant. When she holds Lemongrass Spa parties, she tells everyone that she had no family history of cancer, was a vegetarian, and never drank, smoked, or used drugs. She exercised and breastfed her kids. Even though Donna did all the "right things," she still got cancer.

While Donna's doctors said that she will never know for sure what caused the cancer, she wonders if culprits could have been pollutants in the air and chemicals in skin care products.

"I could drive myself crazy trying to figure it out," Donna said. "Or I could make a choice to control what I can, such as my diet, skin-care, and makeup. I feel empowered because I was able to change the products that I use in an effort to stop my cancer from returning."

"Don't wait till you have the problem," Donna said. "Make changes to your life now so that you won't get the diagnosis you don't want."

Taking a Natural Approach

As a naturopathic physician in Enfield, Connecticut, it was a given that Amy Rothenberg, 54 at the time, would turn to naturopathic medicine to go along with conventional cancer care when she faced both breast cancer and ovarian cancer in the same year.

Amy knew it wasn't a good sign when she found a lump in her breast on New Year's Day in 2014. She had never had fibrous breasts, and she has a strong family history of breast and ovarian cancer. Within a week, she learned that the lump was cancer.

After getting a second opinion and considering her options, Amy chose to have a double mastectomy and reconstructive surgery, which was followed by chemotherapy and radiation treatment because the tumor in her breast was showing signs of spreading. Three weeks after finishing treatment for breast cancer, Amy learned she had ovarian cancer that required another surgery and more chemo.

Throughout her year of surgeries and cancer treatments, Amy used naturopathic medicine to prevent side effects of the treatment and to address those side effects that did arise. It helped give her the energy to keep dancing, cook healthy meals, take walks, and go to the gym. She also took time off from work to focus on healing and preparing the foods she knew were best for her at the time.

Amy weathered the year with the help of family and friends, including her husband and three adult children. She wrote about her experiences on her blog, Field Notes for Natural Medicine (DrAmyRothenberg.Blogspot.com), and for the *Huffington Post* (http://www.huffingtonpost.com/author/amy-rothenberg-nd). Amy approached her treatment with a commitment to healthy eating and lowering her stress level through yoga, mindful meditation, and other techniques.

An important note: Amy saw a naturopathic physician colleague for care during her cancer treatment, and she recommends trying naturopathic medicine on your own. It's particularly helpful to see a doctor who practices naturopathic oncology. You can find one through the Oncology Association of Naturopathic Physicians (OncANP.org).

"An expert will help address supplements, diet, exercise, and stress reduction, taking into account your overall health and health history," Amy said.

Amy started her therapy before her first surgery. She took probiotics and ate cultured foods to help diversify and make more robust bacterial flora in her gut, ate animal protein to promote tissue healing, and focused on foods rich in antioxidants that help fight cancer, including mushrooms, berries, and other fruits and vegetables. She spent her days prior to surgery cooking healthy, nutritious meals and freezing them to have during recovery.

Hydration was also important before and after surgery and throughout her cancer treatments, so Amy drank plenty of water

> *"Cancer can take away all of my physical abilities. It cannot touch my mind, it cannot touch my heart, and it cannot touch my soul."*
>
> —JIM VALVANO

and tea, and she ate foods that contain lots of water, such as fruits, vegetables, and soups.

After Amy's surgery, she took nutritional supplements to improve her immune function. She also ate a "clean" diet that included juices, vegetables, fruits, lean protein, and cultured foods such as miso, yogurt, and fermented vegetables. She was mindful of keeping refined sugars, alcohol, and any foods that don't normally agree with her out of her diet.

She avoided opioid painkillers after surgery by instead using homeopathic medicines and remedies prescribed by her naturopathic physician. She also addressed pain through acupuncture, acupressure, and massage, which help reduce inflammation and promote healing.

"Healing happens when you give yourself time, proper nutrients, and rest," Amy said.

Amy also exercised as she was able because enhanced circulation from exercise also promotes healing. She started walking laps around her house, then she walked to her mailbox and back, until she could go to the gym for gentle walking on the treadmill and a return to weight lifting.

"When you exercise, you enhance perfusion of the blood to all parts of your body," Amy said. "Anticancer approaches will be amplified if you're well exercised."

> *Healing is a matter of time, but it is sometimes also a matter of opportunity.*
>
> HIPPOCRATES

When it was time for radiation treatment, Amy always spent an hour walking before her appointment, which has been shown to increase efficacy of radiation treatments.

In addition to eating healing foods, exercising, and taking nutritional supplements, Amy practiced positive thinking, addressed anxiety and worries, and kept a sense of humor.

"Your mental game is most important," Amy said.

Amy tried to normalize her life as much as possible by getting out of the house, going out for a meal, and socializing.

Amy didn't have much nausea during her chemo treatments. Conventional anti-nausea medication helped. She also ate rice pudding and drank ginger tea, in addition to taking supplements known to enhance chemo sensitivity of cancer cells and to prevent side effects of chemo.

She felt tired during this time but not extremely fatigued. That may be because she fasted for four days at a time during her chemo treatment to deprive cancer cells of nutrients. She thinks it helped improve her energy level.

"I don't recommend calorie restriction during chemo for everyone," Amy cautioned.

At the very end of her treatment, Amy had a setback. One day, after yoga, Amy tripped getting off of her yoga mat. She fell, landing on her arm, which caused a very painful hematoma, a collection of blood in the tissue, where it doesn't belong.

"I had a lot of pain at the end of a very tough year," Amy said.

The injury temporarily stopped her from doing things she loved, including walking, yoga, and dance. But she had honed a set of skills for reducing worry and anxiety, including stopping negative thoughts, expressing gratitude, and using positive visualization.

"Those skills are great to use in a pinch," Amy said. "But they only work in a pinch if you practice them."

Amy said she went into cancer treatment at the top of her game: happy, healthy, and strong. She ended strong too. Just four months after finishing her last treatment, she completed her first triathlon.

Part 5

STAYING BRAVE— DESPITE ADVERSITY

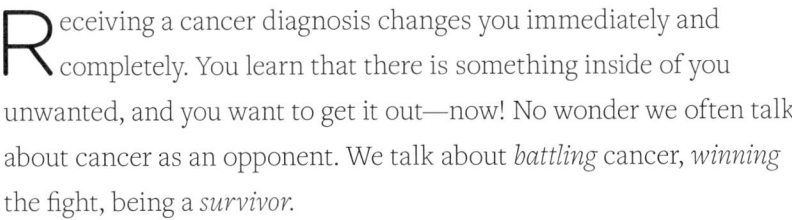

Receiving a cancer diagnosis changes you immediately and completely. You learn that there is something inside of you unwanted, and you want to get it out—now! No wonder we often talk about cancer as an opponent. We talk about *battling* cancer, *winning* the fight, being a *survivor*.

Even though fighting cancer is a battle no one signs up for, a battle we wish we didn't have to fight, we know instinctively it will require bravery to win. Bravery against cancer can have many faces. In an act of quiet bravery, a mom looks away to shield her children from her tears. A husband finds the courage to have one more treatment to make sure that his cancer is truly gone. A woman encourages her sister to have a mammogram, even though it's the last thing she wants to think about. A grandmom proudly goes out in public sans hair, and even sans hat to show her strength. These images, and more, are the many faces of bravery.

Bravery is about summoning inner courage, strength, optimism, and fortitude. It's what you draw on when you think you have nothing else to give. But you do.

Your outlook as you walk a cancer journey is so important. In 2010, the *Journal of Thoracic Oncology* published the results of a study exploring the impact of lung cancer patients' outlook when it comes to their illness. According to the study, patients with optimistic attitudes were more likely to live longer. Both men and women who were classified in the study as patients with optimistic attitudes survived an average of six months longer than people with negative outlooks. The five-year survival rate for optimists was almost 33 percent, compared with only 21 percent of pessimists.

Deep inside of you there's a strength you had no idea you had, a courage beyond belief, and a bravery that might surprise even you.

Taking Time to Re-Focus

On September 11, 2001, Gary Pack, now 73, of Bailey, Colorado, went to see his doctor for the results of a routine physical exam. His doctor said that his chest X-ray showed a small spot on his left lung that was probably nothing.

"But we will need to keep an eye on it," the doctor said.

An hour later, the whole world changed when the twin towers went down.

Gary put the "spot" far in the back of his mind.

Fast-forward to 2006. Time for another routine physical. Again *the spot* came up. Gary, a retired corporate executive, was put on a schedule for a CT (computerized tomography) scan of his lungs every six months "to keep an eye on it."

Two years later, the spot had grown a little, so Gary's doctor did a biopsy. That's when they found a neuroendocrine tumor, which in Gary's case was cancerous. It's a rare form of cancer that, in Gary's case at least, was very slow growing. That was the good news. The bad news: There's no cure.

> *"It is during our darkest moments that we must focus to see the light."*
>
> —ARISTOTLE

That October, Gary had surgery to remove the upper lobe of his left lung. Six months after the surgery, the symptoms came back, primarily toxic hot flushing in the middle of the night, but the tumors from metastasis, or spread, of this type of cancer are too small to locate and may or may not take years to develop. Gary developed several blood clots after surgery, which necessitated a 10-day stay in the hospital. The medication he was taking caused his gallbladder to fail, which had to be removed.

"Other than that, physically I was doing great," Gary said.

But because there's no cure for this type of cancer, Gary wondered how great he was going to be *mentally*. Specifically, how would he keep his mind occupied—and off of worries about the cancer?

"I feared that I might just sit around waiting for it to get worse," Gary said. "I read online that the average survival was five years from diagnosis."

Needing a major distraction, Gary took up photography—never mind he had no experience and was starting at ground zero.

"I approached learning photography with 'an imminent sense of urgency,'" Gary said. "That's a phrase I learned in business school meaning *approach it like you have a fixed period of time, not a lifetime, to get it right*. I jumped in with both feet, buying the best equipment I could afford so there would be no excuse but 'operator error' for a bad shot."

Gary spent hours and hours on the Internet studying and learning.

He shot hundreds of photos and analyzed each one to determine why it did or did not work, and in the process, he became a better and better photographer. He joined a great camera club and some Internet photo critique sites.

"I found a *passion and joy* that will continue to grow for the rest of my life," Gary said. "Whether it's the sheer exhilaration of being there at that moment in time to witness the beauty of the scene or the adrenaline rush of being 20 miles up a dirt road completely alone in the silence, I love every minute of it."

What Gary has grown to love most about photography is that there's always something to learn and an opportunity to get "better." There's no waking up one morning and thinking, *I'm as good as I'm going to get.* "I have yet to take my best photograph," he likes to say.

"I make learning something new every day a top priority," Gary said. "I feel my very best when I'm out taking/making pictures, when I am in what I call the photo-zone. Experts say you can't feel both a positive and negative emotion or reaction at the same time. I'm so focused on what I'm doing and loving it to the extent that, while in that zone anyway, I give no thought to anything carcinoid. I have my bad times later in the evening and in the middle of the night."

Gary chooses every day what he's going to focus on, and it's *not* cancer. His landscape photography is now for sale at a local art gallery where he also works part-time.

"Every day, I look forward to learning something new and getting better at it," Gary said. "It's all about what I put in the forefront of my life."

Wearing Her Baldness Proudly

When Billie Jean Patton was 20 years old, she found a lump in her breast. It was removed, and fortunately it was found to be benign.

But unfortunately that was only the first of many lumps that Billie Jean would have to contend with over the next 35 years of her life. Most of the lumps were at least aspirated, a procedure in which fluid is drawn from the mass with a long needle, and some of them even needed to be removed. But time after time, all of the lumps were found to be benign—nuisances all.

For all of those years, Billie Jean, now 57 years old and an office manager with Three Rivers School District in Grants Pass, Oregon, had been religious about having yearly mammograms. But like so many things in life, clean mammo after clean mammo lulled her into a false sense of security.

Life got busy, and Billie Jean missed one test. Then she missed another. She continued to do monthly self-exams at home, though.

> "*Learn from yesterday. Live for today. Hope for tomorrow.*"
>
> —ALBERT EINSTEIN

But even when she found a lump during a self-exam, she wasn't overly worried.

"Here we go again," Billie Jean thought. "My lumpy girls have another one."

But this one hurt.

That was new. So Billie Jean scheduled a mammogram for August 11, 2016.

The following day, Billie received the diagnosis: invasive ductal carcinoma, estrogen and progesterone positive but HER2 negative. She was absolutely shocked.

"I would have never in a million years thought I would get cancer. My family history has plenty of heart disease and high blood pressure, but no cancer," Billie Jean said. "I was terrified that I was going to die."

Billie Jean went to several doctor's appointments for information, tests, and recommendations.

"I was told that if you have breast cancer, this is the one you want to have," Billie Jean said. "Yes, it is cancer. Yes, it is serious. But yes, it is *survivable*."

On October 5, Billie Jean had a partial mastectomy. The surgeon removed a tennis-ball-size mass and five lymph nodes. The surgeon explained that Billie Jean's cancer was stage 3 advanced. Her doctor recommended following up the surgery with chemotherapy and radiation. Although initially Billie Jean's case was borderline, after receiving an updated diagnosis after surgery, she knew she had no choice but to have both treatments to reduce her chances of having a recurrence.

Despite many possible side effects, the only one that has really affected Billie Jean is hair loss.

"My hair was falling out, so I buzzed my head to get it over with quickly," she said. "A close friend buzzed it for me, and his wife held my hand while I cried. But it was okay. Now I wear my baldness proudly. I wear it for all of the women who are terrified to let other people see them without a wig or a hat."

Billie Jean is still going through her treatments, and she is doing well, grateful to have a strong body that is tolerating the medications so well.

"I am now cancer-free," she said.

And she's determined to stay that way. She has made dietary changes to reduce her risk of recurrence. Because her type of cancer is hormone-driven, she eats a low-soy, low-fat, and low-sugar diet. She will also take a hormone blocker for up to 10 years.

"I've made peace with the idea of dying," Billie Jean said. "Now I do my best to live day-to-day, instead of projecting or worrying about how many days I have left. I don't have a bucket list, but I spend as much time with my family as I can. I'm learning how to be grateful for the little things in life."

Courageously Choosing to Live

Five years ago, Lourdes Fitzgerald was feeling great. The retired call center manager, who lives in Chicago, Illinois, ate well and exercised. She even made it a point to sleep the "right" amount of time each night.

Lourdes, who's now 62 years old and a mom of two grown children and a foster son, had been noticing her stool getting skinnier and skinner, however. She had a thought that something wasn't quite right, but she wasn't very worried about it.

One day in May 2012, an unexpected phone call changed her life.

The nurse at Lourdes's doctor's office—which was a little slow that time of year—called to say, "We haven't seen you in a while. Would you want to come in for a checkup?" At the time, Lourdes's life was anything but slow. She was always on the go, always "pushing the envelope" to do more, faster, better.

Yet, because of that nagging feeling caused by the change in her stool, Lourdes made the time to go to the doctor. She went in as requested for that checkup.

> *The greatest healing therapy is friendship and love.*
>
> HUBERT H. HUMPHREY

Thank goodness.

Lourdes's doctor was also concerned about the change in her stool. He referred her to a gastroenterologist for her first colonoscopy. Prior to that, her insurance company had covered only routine tests of her stool samples. The colonoscopy revealed a tumor in the lower part of her colon.

"I was shocked," Lourdes remembered. "I wasn't expecting that at all."

The doctor diagnosed Lourdes with stage 2 colon cancer. Unfortunately, when the surgeon operated on Lourdes to remove the tumor, he found that the cancer had spread. Rather than being stage 2 as the gastroenterologist had thought, it was stage 4. The cancer had spread to Lourdes's liver and also to her lungs.

After having surgery to remove the tumor, Lourdes needed to have six weeks of chemotherapy and radiation. She's been on weekly chemo ever since—a maintenance dose if the cancer hasn't grown or a full dose if it has.

Lourdes's biggest challenge has been the nausea and vomiting from the chemo. After a treatment, the nausea and vomiting can be intense. Then it eases slowly as the week goes along, only to have the cycle repeat again after the next chemo treatment.

A key for Lourdes to make it through has been eating and drinking enough to keep up her strength.

"When I don't feel well, I just sit around, not really doing anything," Lourdes said. "I feel like I'm wasting my life! I don't want to do that. I'd rather *live*!"

So Lourdes tries her best to eat and drink.

"I can't stand water!" Lourdes said. To her, water tastes really bad, which is another side effect of the chemo. Lourdes is able to drink it, however, when she mixes water with something else, such as iced tea.

Drinking plenty of her water-tea combo also helps to ease another side effect of the chemo—constipation.

Lourdes has used trial and error to find foods that she can keep down. Campbell's bean soup is usually a winner.

After her diagnosis, Lourdes made some changes to her life. Because the chemo can weaken her bones, she takes weekly yoga classes to maintain her bone density.

But what has helped Lourdes the most through her diagnosis and treatment is the support and love of her family.

"When I was diagnosed, I reached out to all of my family," Lourdes remembers.

"We are very close, and we keep in good contact."

Lourdes told them each about her diagnosis. She shared how tough the surgery and treatments have been on her. One by one, Lourdes's family promised to pray for her.

"They relayed their sympathy and their concerns to me," Lourdes said. "That really helped me a lot. Many of them have said that I'm an inspiration to them because I'm so strong. They say that they look up to me. They say that they don't think they could have made it through all that I have. That makes me feel really good. They are actually an inspiration to *me*."

And so, it's become a circle of inspiration: Lourdes serves as an inspiration to her friends and family, and their expressions of inspiration help her to carry on her fight.

Bravely Accepting Help

Some cancers don't present themselves with obvious symptoms. They are vastly more difficult to diagnose.

This was the case when Denise Treml, 49, was diagnosed with non-Hodgkin's lymphoma. Despite a few aches and pains—which Denise attributed to getting older—she felt fine. She was a single mother, enjoying a busy life with her two children—Madison, who's now 18, and Jeremy, who's now 16.

Denise had worked hard all of her life, holding down two jobs from the time she was a teenager until she hit 30. In addition to working full-time, Denise was involved in her children's activities, and she even took care of her ill mother.

In 2015, Denise went for her annual physical. Everything came back perfect—even her blood work.

Because of a little nagging back pain, Denise went to weekly treatments with a chiropractor. One week, Denise's chiropractor thought that there was something "just not right" with her back. She

> *"When you come to the end of your rope, tie a knot and hang on."*
>
> —FRANKLIN D. ROOSEVELT

suggested that Denise get a magnetic resonance imaging (MRI) scan of her back.

Denise followed the chiropractor's advice, and she went to her primary care physician to order the test. When Denise received the results, she Googled all of the medical jargon.

That's when Denise realized that she may have cancer.

Denise met with her chiropractor, and together they reviewed the results. Even though Denise had already read the report, and she had time to process the seriousness of her diagnosis, she still felt devastated to hear the chiropractor say it aloud: It may be cancer.

The chiropractor showed Denise two large masses visible on the MRI scan; they were located exactly where she was experiencing the back pain. Although non-Hodgkin's lymphoma is a blood cancer, it invades the lymphatic system, and it causes tumor-like masses to develop throughout the body. Denise was referred to an oncologist, and a biopsy was done a week later, which confirmed the diagnosis: stage 4 nonfollicular non-Hodgkins lymphoma.

Denise was told that her type of cancer was not curable, but it *was* treatable. For the rest of her life, after the initial aggressive treatment, she will need to be monitored closely and kept on a maintenance dose of chemotherapy.

Denise was referred to an oncologist for treatment. In June 2015, she began aggressive chemotherapy.

After six months of the initial treatment, Denise's scans showed her tumors were reduced in size by 40 percent. Unfortunately, this exciting news was short lived. Denise's next scan showed that the medication was no longer working. Her oncologist decided to put her on a maintenance oral dose of chemotherapy to see if it would work. Thankfully, this has been helping, and today Denise is doing well.

Part of staying brave through cancer is having the strength to reach out for help. Denise's boyfriend, John Shaw, was one of her biggest supporters. He has never missed a doctor's appointment or chemo treatment. He is always there, along with her two children, giving her unconditional support.

Denise has also found support from a national organization with local chapters, called Cancer Support Community (CSC). In addition to group therapy, CSC offers seminars with guest speakers on relevant cancer topics, yoga classes that focus on relaxing the mind and body, and other beneficial activities for cancer patients. Denise used to need to travel an hour to visit a group, but they're opening a local affiliate in her hometown of Middletown, Delaware. To learn more about them, visit CancerSupportCommunity.org.

Denise's battle with cancer also brings into focus the harsh reality of the financial strains the disease puts on patients and their families. Denise kept working during her chemotherapy treatment from June of 2015 until September of 2016. Despite experiencing extreme exhaustion during chemo, she managed to simultaneously undergo treatment and work full-time for more than a year. The burden finally became too much to bear, though, and Denise had to leave her job.

"I always try to look at the big picture," Denise said. "I never let the little negative things get me down. Keeping a positive mindset is most important in fighting this disease."

Returning to Her Glorious Mediocrity

Barbara Weiss described her life pre-cancer as "gloriously mediocre." Barbara and her husband were empty nesters with two grown children, living in Wilmington, Delaware. Barbara's husband had just semi-retired, and she was still working full-time as an office manager.

Barbara enjoyed a simple life, taking walks and working in her garden. She had always been blessed with good health. Like many of us, Barbara didn't keep up with regular visits to her physician and her mammograms.

Because Barbara had always been in good health, she had the "not me" attitude in regards to getting sick. She was a private person to boot.

"I always hated going to the doctor for anything," Barbara said.

The thought of a stranger, even a medical professional, touching and probing at her breasts made Barbara uncomfortable. Because Barbara had lumpy breasts all of her life, she wasn't alarmed about feeling a lump or two. As a result, Barbara never had a mammogram—

until one day, when Barbara was 58, she noticed a painful red lesion on the outside of one of her breasts.

On June 30, 2011, Barbara gathered up her courage and set aside her fears. She visited her primary doctor to have the lesion examined. After examining the lesion, Barbara's doctor referred her immediately to the Helen Graham Cancer Center. Really immediately, as in that afternoon.

Barbara knew for certain that the situation was serious because the folks at the Helen Graham Cancer Center immediately expedited her into a meeting with a surgeon. Before the lesion was even biopsied, the surgeon told her that it was cancer.

Next, Barbara underwent a battery of exams and tests. Her final diagnosis a week later? Stage 3B breast cancer.

Barbara had always heard about cancer treatments that caused months of vomiting, weakness, and pain. The treatment of cancer seemed inhumane to her.

"I had always thought to myself, *If I am ever diagnosed with cancer, I would certainly skip all of that*," Barbara said.

But when Barbara was suddenly confronted with her own diagnosis and mortality, her viewpoint changed. In an instant. She was now willing to do absolutely anything that her doctors wanted to try. Her newfound bravery was borne out of that diagnosis that very day.

"I now joke that I was told I would receive injections of potentially lethal drugs, have body parts lopped off, and receive hazardous amounts of radiation," Barbara said. "My response? Sign me up!"

Blessed with a loving family and friends, Barbara bravely took on the challenge of beating cancer. Her husband sat with her through all of her chemotherapy treatments. Her friends called regularly and sent her cards she would cherish forever.

> *"We have two options, medically and emotionally: Give up or fight like hell."*
>
> —LANCE ARMSTRONG

Barbara found that her cancer treatments weren't as torturous as she had feared. She even managed to work through her treatments because she tolerated them so well. Cancer treatment has come a long way with improved drugs and procedures. Depending on the type of cancer and the treatments required, a lot of people are able to maintain active lifestyles during treatment.

Barbara is also a 30-year member of a 12-step program. This lady knows the strength of a higher power! Barbara used the faith, wisdom, and spiritual guidance she learned from this program to overcome the challenge of cancer in her life.

Barbara and her husband are no strangers to fighting cancer. Barbara's experience was their second time going through this because her husband was diagnosed with prostate cancer in 2008. She vowed to be a survivor just like him.

Like all cancer patients, Barbara had a lot of emotions to work through.

"I was scared to death!" Barbara said.

A lot of this fear was rooted in Barbara's prior perceptions of cancer. She grew up in an era where the "C" word meant death.

"When I was a little girl, people with cancer had little hope of survival," Barbara said. "When I got my diagnosis, I felt confronted with my own mortality."

This brought on feelings of guilt about not getting regular mammograms. Barbara recognizes the importance of going for mammograms, saying that her cancer could have been diagnosed earlier and her treatment time could have been shorter.

But because there's no changing the past, Barbara has learned to forgive herself. Now she concentrates on a healthy future.

Barbara didn't just make changes to her philosophy on the importance of getting mammograms done. She found a new appreciation for the "normalcy" of everyday living.

"When I was diagnosed and going through treatment, the thing that I most yearned for was normalcy," Barbara said.

There's a chance that Barbara's cancer will return, and the treatments she received could lead to other problems. However, Barbara gives good advice on how to handle these fears.

"Sometimes I'm vulnerable to these scary possibilities," Barbara said. "But I don't linger in those thoughts. I remind myself to live in the moment, and the moment is usually good."

With all of Barbara's treatments behind her, she has returned to her normal life. She's back to her "glorious mediocrity."

Focusing on What She Could Keep

The year that Amy Carpenter turned 40 was a busy one—just like any year for a mother of four. Amy's children—Joshua, 8, Elizabeth, 10, Daniel, 12 and Anna, 14—all needed help with different after-school activities and homework assignments.

Amy also worked part-time as a substitute teacher, and she was taking care of a foster child. So much was going on in the family that Amy decided to wait a few months before she got her first mammogram.

One day, in April of 2015, Amy felt a lump in her breast. It was just a few month before her first scheduled mammogram.

Amy went to her appointment as planned. She was shocked to receive her diagnosis: stage 4 metastatic breast cancer, which meant that the cancer had spread to other organs. Amy learned that the cancer had spread into her liver and possibly even into her bones.

The doctors didn't delay giving Amy their treatment plan. Along with chemotherapy, Amy would need a partial mastectomy and reconstructive surgery.

"Faith: It does not make things easy; it makes them possible."

—ANONYMOUS

When Amy was diagnosed, she didn't jump to conclusions or worry about all the "what ifs."

"I believed in my faith in God," Amy said. "I knew that He had this all under control."

During this time, Amy leaned heavily on her support group from church. She had a strong faith before cancer, and it helped her through this difficult time.

"I also vowed not to focus on what cancer was going to take away from me," Amy said. "Instead, my focus was on what I was going to *keep*."

Time with Amy's family was one of the most important things that she planned on keeping.

It seems counter-intuitive, but Amy decided to switch treatment centers to the University of Michigan. Even though that would require Amy to drive 70 minutes each way for her treatments, she felt it was the right decision for her because there they deal with many patients with her type of cancer, and it's also a major cancer research center.

"Working with these experienced doctors was a proactive way for me to extend my quality of life and to give me more time with my family," Amy said. "The long drive is worth it to me to work with healthcare professionals that specialize in my type of cancer."

For serious conditions, going to a hospital network that specializes in your condition can really make a difference in your recovery time and treatment options. You'll be receiving the latest in technological and medical breakthroughs and working with doctors with the most experience treating your condition.

A challenge that Amy faced right away was how to tell her family about her diagnosis. Because Amy's children ranged in ages from 8 to 14 years old, each one had a different understanding of the disease. Amy and her husband, Frank, took time to explain to the children the type of cancer their mom had and how it would be treated. They found that the children's questions and concerns varied according to their age. For example, their son Joshua, 8, didn't understand that his mother would be losing one of her breasts. It wasn't until Amy's prosthetic breast came in the mail, from an organization called Knitted Knockers, that Joshua made this connection.

Knitted Knockers is an amazing organization providing knitted prosthetic breast while breast cancer patients are waiting for their reconstructive surgery. To learn more about Knitted Knockers, visit them at KnittedKnockers.org.

"Through my entire treatment process, my husband and I have worked hard to support our children," Amy said. "We offer honest answers to questions and concerns while keeping the conversations age appropriate."

Amy had a challenging road ahead of her with a stage 4-breast cancer diagnosis. During the month before treatment started, she also needed staging surgery. Staging surgery helps doctors plan the best treatment options and gives the patient a more accurate prognosis. It also gives doctors the tumor size, location and whether it has grown into other locations. In Amy's case, they were checking if it had spread to the lymph nodes. Unfortunately, it had spread to the lymphatic system, and she needed to have the lymph nodes on the left side of her breast removed.

As a result of losing the lymph nodes on her left side, Amy suffers from lymphedema in her left arm. This is a condition that causes swelling in the arms or legs that can happen after lymph nodes are removed.

To help with the swelling, Amy wraps her arm in a compression bandage. To soothe her skin, she applies Lemongrass Spa Healing Elements Balm first. She also has used it on her surgical scars.

Because Amy's tumor was so large, her doctors treated her with four months of chemotherapy before attempting surgery. After the chemo, the tumor had shrunk enough to do a partial mastectomy of her left breast. Amy then had reconstructive surgery in December of 2016.

"I put that surgery off until the winter so I could go camping and hiking with my children in the summer," Amy said. "It's so important to make every moment count."

The type of cancer that Amy has can never be cured, but it *can* be managed. Today, Amy's doctors say she has NED, which means No Evidence of Disease. This is the new phrase in cancer used in place of "remission."

Amy has happily returned to most of the activities that she enjoyed pre-cancer: taking care of her family, staying active, and returning to teaching. She will need to be closely monitored for any new cancer developments.

"But if so, then we'll just find a new treatment plan," Amy said.

Fighting to Survive

We use a lot of empowering words to describe cancer patients. They are warriors, fighters, and survivors. Among all these words there is one that word that ties them all together and that word is *bravery*. In order to beat cancer, one must be brave to fight and survive. Paige Sharrer, age 44, from Royersford, Pennsylvania, is one of the bravest warriors cancer has ever come up against. Twice in her life, once when she was 16 and then again when she was 37, she had cancer of two different types.

When Paige was 16, she was diagnosed with Hodgkin's Lymphoma, which is a type of cancer that develops from cells in the lymphatic system. Then at 37 Paige was diagnosed with breast cancer. Through all of her surgeries and treatments, she never stopped fighting and was determined to participate in activities she enjoyed. Her ability to stay strong through these two difficult battles against cancer is an inspiration.

Before Paige's first diagnosis at 16 with Hodgkin's Lymphoma, her life was like most high school students. She was busy in sports, school activities, and dating. She was hardly ever sick, except for one day at school when she didn't feel well and was sent home to rest. When she woke up, she had a large lump on her neck by her collarbone. Her parents took her to the doctor to get it checked out. After all the diagnostic tests were done, her parents sat her down and gave her the bad news. Like most 16 year olds, Paige had no idea what Hodgkin's Lymphoma was. When she learned it was cancer, a flood of emotions overcame her:

"I was completely shocked, scared, and confused," Paige remembers. "I wondered how that could be true!"

Paige's parents found the best oncologist to treat her cancer. The first step was to have a procedure known as a staging laparotomy. This allows doctors to take samples of tissue to test how far the cancer has spread. In Paige's case, the procedure was extremely invasive.

"I had a scar that was a little over a foot long down my stomach," Paige said. "I was devastated."

At any age, scaring like this is difficult to deal with, but as a high school aged student, it made Paige feel even more different than her peers. This would be just the beginning of cancer interrupting her young life. Her treatment involved radiation treatments that made her too ill to attend school. When she was finally well enough to return to classes, the treatments had left her with skin burns, including some on parts of her face. She was teased by her classmates about this and the fact that special accommodations had to be made for her.

"I was teased a lot in school," Paige said. "I had to be dismissed from classes early so that I wasn't jostled in the hall, because I was still recovering from surgery, which drew even more unwanted attention. After a while the hair started to fall out of the back of my head and with this more teasing came. I was completely depressed and scared."

Paige's treatment was successful, but there were complications from the radiation treatments she needed in order to save her life. She struggled with eating because the radiation had done so much damage to her digestive system. It became a struggle for her to maintain her weight. At one point, Paige needed a feeding tube to nourish her body. The radiation had also done damage to Paige's thyroid gland, bones, and lungs.

Through all these complications, Paige persevered. She earned her nursing degree and has been a critical care nurse since 1999. She also started a family and is a proud mother of her son, who's now 13.

Then another crisis hit.

In 2009, Paige was busy working, training Brazilian Jiu Jitsu, and of course raising her son. She was also recently engaged and was hoping to wear a strapless wedding gown. She looked into getting a breast lift because her first battle with lymphoma left her with so much weight loss in her chest. As a precaution, the surgeon asked her to get a mammogram before the operation. It was a little early for her to get one because they are not recommended until age 40, but she agreed to have the test done. After her mammogram, Paige knew the news wasn't good when her surgeon finally asked her to come in and meet in his office.

"I received another dreaded phone call from my surgeon saying that he would open his office (it was a Sunday) to talk to me. I knew then that it could only be bad news. So I met with him and realized that my nightmare was back."

Paige learned she had breast cancer.

She ended up having a bilateral mastectomy with tissue expanders placed for future reconstructive surgery. To follow would be more surgeries and medications necessary for Paige to regain her health.

Paige's fiancé at the time couldn't deal with her cancer on a physical or an emotional level. They ended up breaking up, the wedding was cancelled, and Paige had to move back in with her mother for some time. She was also separated from her son because he was attending school an hour away while she was undergoing the cancer therapies.

After all that cancer had taken from her, Paige had every reason to be angry and resentful, but instead she said, "The positive way it changed my life is that it gave me a strong sense of fight. I refused to quit and was determined to overcome anything that stood in the way of me getting back to the life I loved. It took a long time, but I did just that. I went from not being able to get out of bed by myself, to being able to temporarily return to Jiu Jitsu, returning to work, taking care of my son, and getting back to the gym."

After breaking off her engagement, Paige was reunited with her first love, whom she met at age 12 and dated on and off throughout high school. They were married in 2011. Paige calls him "her strength."

Today Paige still struggles with the many side effects from her cancer treatments, but she is thankful for all that she has overcome.

"I love my job, my husband, my son, and nature," Paige says. "Because I work in a trauma ICU, I see every day how much worse things could be. I am truly grateful for all I have."

Savoring the Sweet

When life gives you lemons, you might be surprised to find that lemons aren't nearly as bitter as you had feared.

That's what Holly Shoup-Bruch, now 41, discovered on her cancer journey.

Holly, a project manager at an environmental engineering firm, who lives in Saylorsburg, Pennsylvania, led her life in the fast lane.

Literally.

Holly commuted over two hours—each way—to work. Her husband had a *three*-hour commute. They were glad to get home each night to spend time with their now eight-year-old daughter. Fortunately, Holly's parents live with them, offering a lot of help and support—and babysitting!

"We live in a big, mixed generational house," Holly said.

Holly was always grateful for her parents' company, support, and help. But a few years ago, she had no idea the extent she would need to lean on them.

A few years ago, Holly's life was zipping along when she noticed a rash on her left breast.

"I tried applying some topical creams to the rash, and it would come and go," Holly remembered. "I did regular breast self-exams, and I started checking constantly—almost compulsively. Something just didn't feel right to me. It wasn't a lump. But I noticed a change in the density of my breast tissue."

Holly also noticed an aching pain under her arm. She mentioned both symptoms to her ob-gyn. Because Holly was only 38, she hadn't yet had her 40-year-old baseline mammogram.

"You're right," the ob-gyn said, during Holly's exam. "It *does* feel different .But it doesn't seem like something that would be malignant."

With the extra cautiousness common among doctors, the ob-gyn sent Holly for an ultrasound. Because the results of that ultrasound were concerning, her doctor ordered a diagnostic mammogram.

The diagnostic mammogram results were so concerning that her physician ordered an immediate needle biopsy. In fact, they had to do three of them.

"When the nurse came in and asked me to pick a surgeon, I knew things were really going south," Holly said.

What followed was a whirlwind of appointments—with oncologists, radiologists, and the infusion center. Oddly, Holly finally got her diagnosis in an offhand comment by her surgeon, who thought she had already been told.

It was stage 3 estrogen/progesterone positive breast cancer.

"It all happened so quickly," Holly said. "I just wanted to tell everyone, 'Please just slow down!' I was in a state of shock for a few days."

Then, suddenly, a bravery Holly that didn't know she had kicked in.

"I started to calmly think *Okay, if this is the way that it is, then how are we going to get through it?*" Holly said. "I knew that dwelling on my situation and being upset weren't going to get me anywhere good."

Holly had genetic testing, and then a double mastectomy followed by reconstructive surgery. She was out of work, on part-time disability. As soon as she healed from her surgeries, she started chemotherapy.

"I was doing so well on it that I went back to work," Holly said.

But then, out of nowhere, a curve ball hit. Holly developed a severe allergy to the chemo drug. Her doctors switched her to a new drug. It didn't go well.

"I felt like I had been hit by a Mack truck," Holly said. "I was very fortunate to be able to stay home and that I had so much support and help from my parents and friends."

Holly remembers it as a very rough time. The thing that she feels got her through? Her attitude.

"I made a lot of big attitude changes," Holly said. "Cancer teaches you to prioritize things. I used to be a worrier. But after surviving cancer, the small things don't matter to me anymore. Cancer puts it all into perspective."

When most people think of cancer, they think of the many treatments—and those treatments' side effects. Perhaps it was due to Holly's brave attitude, but she experienced that quite differently.

"When you have cancer treatments and procedures, you go through a lot of physical changes," Holly explained. "I was very surprised by the number of *positive* changes I had from chemo. People kept telling me over and over how good I looked! 'You look better and healthier now!' they'd say. When I look back on the pictures taken of me back then, even *I* think I looked pretty good for having cancer!"

Although Holly isn't sure why that was the case, she suspects that having a break from her job and very long commute—and the resulting break from stress—might have played a part.

Like many people undergoing cancer treatments, Holly lost her hair. One of her best friends, who's also a stylist, came to Holly's house to cut her hair short.

"I thought to myself *I've had short hair before. It will grow back*!" Holly said.

Once Holly's hair had mostly all fallen out, she shaved her head.

"I used a lint roller to catch the little bits," Holly said. "Otherwise the stubble would have been falling off everywhere."

Rather than wearing the Metro Beauty Academy wig that Holly had, she wore hats and scarves.

"I had no problem going out with a bald head," she said. "It didn't bother me at all."

That upbeat, positive spirit permeated a lot of Holly's experience.

"It's important to stay positive and take one day at a time," Holly said. "Every day that you make it through is an accomplishment. That's how I got myself through. I counted my treatments down: Only 12 to go, now only 11, now only 10, single digits now, etc. It helped me very much to see the light at the end of the tunnel. If you can see the end, it really helps."

Holly's positive attitude also influenced how she handled her condition with her daughter. Even though Holly's daughter was only five years old when Holly was diagnosed, she chose to share quite a lot about her condition.

"As an only child, my daughter is like a little adult," Holly said. "I knew there was no way I'd go through my surgeries and treatments without her hearing what was going on. I didn't want her worrying or worse, making things up to fill in the blanks of what she might overhear. So I was very upfront with her. I introduced her to my doctors. She came along to many of my treatments. The technicians even showed her how the radiation machine worked."

Holly went through many months of chemo and radiation treatment, with her family by her side.

"My daughter even went along to my last chemo treatment," Holly said. "She helped me to ring the bell after I was finished!"

Part 6

FINDING A WAY
TO GIVE BACK

People have so many remarkably wonderful human traits: kindness, empathy, patience, forgiveness. The connections we feel and the love we share with each other are what makes our journeys so rich and fulfilling.

It's remarkable how often people, even those who have just gone through or are still in the midst of a great challenge, yearn to give back to others. That's the epitome of selfless giving.

Many people find their lives changed after cancer—and not all in a bad way. Cancer can be a powerful teacher, offering lessons of patience, humility, perspective, and gratitude.

Certainly, giving helps other people—whether you volunteer for organizations, offer emotional support to people around you, or donate to charities. But studies show that giving is also good for the *giver*—boosting physical and mental health.

Studies find the following health benefits associated with giving:
- Lower blood pressure
- Increased self-esteem
- Less depression
- Lower stress levels
- Longer life
- Greater happiness

What a wonderful circle of giving to be a part of!

Dressing Up for Chemo

Sometimes, when life hits us the hardest, like with a cancer diagnosis, the best therapy is to give back. The courageous journey of Naomi Ziva, 43, is a perfect example of a cancer survivor living this story.

Before Naomi's diagnosis with colon cancer, she was an active young woman. She loved rock climbing, cycling, and social outings with her friends. Naomi enjoyed her job as a hairdresser, and she lived a happy, single, independent life in Atlanta, Georgia.

When Naomi began experiencing acute pain in her pelvis, she sought out medical attention. At first, her doctors thought she was suffering from pelvic inflammatory disease, which is an infection of a woman's reproductive organs that can lead to infertility.

One night in June of 2016, Naomi's pain was so severe that she had to go to the emergency department. That's where she got the correct diagnosis. Stage 4 colon cancer had spread to Naomi's lungs, liver, and spine.

With this diagnosis—and the impending treatments—Naomi

needed to make swift, sweeping changes to her life. She moved out of her condominium and moved back in with her parents. Having their support was invaluable to Naomi as she started the treatment process.

Naomi began chemotherapy treatments. The pain from the cancer and the chemo weakened Naomi and left her feeling fatigued and weak. On especially bad pain days and after her chemo, she needed to use a walker or wheelchair to get around. All the little things that Naomi used to take for granted in life suddenly became challenges.

Given all of this, it would have been easy for Naomi to retreat into a depression—overwhelmed by feelings of hopelessness. Instead, Naomi decided that the best "medicine" for cancer was laughter and giving to others!

Naomi began taking flowers to her chemo sessions, and she handed them out to all of the other chemotherapy patients. Over the holidays, she gifted the other patients with special treats and candy.

To try to brighten the other patients' day, Naomi started to go to chemo dressed up in costume! Naomi's friend Jennifer always joined her in this adventure. Some days, the friends dressed up as superheroes. Other days, they went as Ginger and Mary Ann from *Gilligan's Island,* as Wayne and Garth from *Wayne's World,* and even as Hulk Hogan and Randy Savage from World Wrestling Entertainment.

"Dressing up for chemo helped me—and I think other patients—face the challenges of these treatments with laughter," Naomi said.

In addition to these activities, Naomi also started a blog, ZivasArmy.Blogspot.com, where she chronicles her fight against cancer. She wanted to create a platform where people diagnosed with cancer and their families and friends could find out what it's actually like *living* with cancer.

"When you're diagnosed with cancer, your doctors will prepare

> *Did I offer peace today? Did I bring a smile to someone's face? Did I say words of healing? Did I let go of my anger and resentment? Did I forgive? Did I love? These are the real questions. I must trust that the little bit of love that I sow now will bear many fruits, here in this world and the life to come.*
>
> — HENRI NOUWEN

and explain your treatment plan," Naomi said. "They go over the side effects of different treatments and surgical procedures. All this is necessary, but people need to know more about the emotional and physical toll that cancer will take on their lives."

In Naomi's eloquently written blog, she takes on this challenge. Cancer patients can relate to and identify with her struggles as they read her blog. Naomi also offers helpful advice and coping skills for patients. She talks about going out dancing with friends on days that she feels good.

"Whenever you can, it's so important to step back into your old life," Naomi said. "You need a chance to forget that you're sick for a while."

This is important advice. A battle with cancer consumes your life. It's important to stay connected to activities and hobbies that you enjoyed pre-cancer.

Naomi has had a long struggle. Her gift of laughter and her willingness to share her story have made living with cancer a more human experience for so many people. There's a tremendous response on Facebook as well as her blog. It has reached all over the world. She's even received feedback from as far away as Israel.

Naomi recently received good news about her condition. The chemotherapy—despite being one of the most challenging parts of her journey—is paying off. Naomi's tumor has been reduced by half the size and has disappeared from her spine. Even though Naomi's own cancer journey won't come to an end any time soon, there is no question that Naomi will continue to give back to the cancer community.

Marching to Help Others

March is colon cancer awareness month. The color for colon cancer awareness is blue. Not many people know these two things. Joey Lydecker, 35, and his wife, Stacey, of Gardendale, Alabama, wish that they didn't either.

Colon cancer hit the couple completely out of the blue—like a bolt of lightning out of a clear blue sky.

Joey was just 34 years old. He worked 12- to 14-hour days on delivery jobs and building furniture. Only married for a few years, the young couple was building their life together.

In early 2016, when Joey started to have pain in his leg, it seemed perfectly logical that he had pulled a muscle. Like they tell medical students: When you hear hoof beats, think horses not zebras.

Who would have imagined the pain would be the first symptom of stage 4 colorectal cancer? Not Joey. Not Stacey. Not even the doctors.

Even when Joey started to have rectal bleeding, the doctors didn't have cancer on their radars. They thought it was hemorrhoids or irritable bowel syndrome.

In March 2016, Joey went to see an orthopedist, who performed a biopsy of his hip bone. That's when Joey was diagnosed with stage 4 colorectal cancer that had already metastasized to his hip. By that time, Joey's pain had gotten so bad that he had to use a walker—sometimes even a wheelchair.

"At 34, you're not expecting that," Joey said. "At least I knew that it was a huge blessing that it hadn't spread to my organs."

Joey underwent 12 rounds of radiation, and then many rounds of chemo infusions. Now he takes a chemo pill and has a chemo pump at home. As time went along, his pain has lessened. On most days now—good days that is—Joey can get around on his own, sans wheelchair or walker.

But the treatments have caused a smorgasbord of side effects. They strike completely unpredictably. Trying to ease them has become an ever-moving target.

"I've had all kinds of side effects," Joey said. "It felt like every week, I was going through something different—diarrhea, nausea, vomiting, insomnia, exhaustion. I'd have one side effect licked, and then a new one would start."

Today, Joey has good days and bad days. A recent CT scan showed "no colorectal mass identified," which means that the main, original tumor is *gone*.

"That means something's working!" Joey said. "The doctors were in shock that they didn't see the tumor at all."

Joey credits a lot of his improvement with his faith in God.

"He has a lot of people praying for him," Stacey said. "Prayer works. God will get you through anything. We have 'let God have it,' let Him take over our struggles, crying out to Him when we needed to."

> *"Courage is not the absence of fear, but rather the judgment that something else is more important than fear."*
>
> —AMBROSE REDMOOM

Today, Joey said, "I feel pretty good. I'm just tired."

Joey and Stacey are helping to get the word out about colorectal cancer—and about the importance of paying attention to your body, talking to your doctor, and getting colonoscopies.

In March, Stacey gave a presentation at their city council meeting about colon cancer awareness month.

"It's commonly believed that risk for colon cancer starts at age 50," Stacey said. "Nowadays, it's much more than a 50-plus disease. It can strike anybody."

"I recommend that if you're having any symptoms, such as rectal bleeding, a change in appetite, or losing weight without trying to, see your doctor," Joey said. "No matter how old you are, ask your doctor to check into it."

"50 is far too late to be screened," Joey said. "Colorectal cancer is being diagnosed in people at younger and younger ages."

According to the Colon Cancer Alliance, colon cancer is 90 percent beatable—when it's caught early.

Helping Her Bosom Buddies

In May of 2016, Laura McCurdy was a 64-year-old active retiree helping with her grandchildren, quilting, and camping. She was always good about getting her yearly mammograms, but that year, like many busy moms and grandmothers, she was late making her appointment.

Laura went for her routine gynecology exam, and the doctor, after her breast exam, inquired if she'd had her mammogram yet this year.

"I knew I was late," Laura said. "But I had planned to go that summer."

The doctor told Laura that she would need to go tomorrow. He had found a lump that was concerning, but told her not to worry at this point. Thankfully, she listened to her doctor and got the mammogram the next day.

Laura stresses the importance of annual checkups with your ob-gyn, breast self-exams, and getting mammograms at the recommended ages. She understands that the mammograms can be

> *"Be strong, be fearless, be beautiful. And believe that anything is possible when you have the right people there to support you."*
>
> —MISTY COPELAND

uncomfortable, but the benefits of early breast cancer detection are invaluable. Catching her cancer in its early stages made the treatment and recovery process much less painful and invasive.

Only eight days after Laura received her breast cancer diagnosis, she had surgery. Her life drastically changed from worrying only about her family to having to worry about herself. This was something she hadn't done in years, but now to continue to be there for her family, she needed to put herself first.

In addition to needing surgery, Laura also needed to have radiation treatments. She was worried about these treatments. In her mind she imagined long, dreadful sessions with visible radiation rays painfully piercing her skin. She had made it through the surgery, and so far all was going smoothly.

After Laura's incision healed, which took about four weeks, it was time for her first radiation treatment. Much to her surprise, the radiation sessions were short and painless, and there were no visible rays. Only toward the end of her therapy did she develop a rash.

"It looked and felt like a sunburn," Laura said. "Once the treatments were finished, my skin returned to normal."

Laura has three adult boys, and they were tremendously supportive throughout her cancer journey. She said sometimes she received up to six calls a day from them. Friends and neighbors were also always checking in, offering to lend a hand.

Laura held up well through her treatments. She really never felt sick and still managed to keep up with her grandchildren, even taking them camping on the weekends. Of course, she had to pace herself, and hiking trips were shorter, but for the most part, it was life as usual for her. From diagnosis to cure, Laura maintained a positive attitude, and her doctors believed this played an important role in her recovery.

The biggest part of Laura's struggle was feeling guilty about how well she was getting through her treatments. She belonged to a local breast cancer support group named Bosom Buddies, and many of her friends had much more troubling stories to tell. When she mentioned her feelings of guilt in a Bosom Buddies meeting, the other survivors helped her realize that every person's struggle is relevant and important to share. Now, Laura uses her experience with breast cancer to help educate other women about the importance of early detection, and to show that some cancer treatments can be tolerated with relatively few side effects.

Laura is now finished with her treatments and is being monitored by her oncologist. She continues to be active with the Bosom Buddies Cancer Support Group, giving back by fundraising and sharing her journey with others. She also still gives her family a high priority, but she has a slightly different mindset these days. She takes care of herself first so she will be here to enjoy them for many more years yet to come.

Going from Customer to Consultant

It was one of the best times in Destinae Nacin's life. She was newly married and enjoying her life with her new husband, Andrew. Destinae was living in Leesburg, Virginia, and working as a kindergarten teacher. Everything in her life was in place.

In January 2016, that all changed. Destinae had her annual checkup. Just three weeks later, she decided to do a self-breast exam in the shower. She found a lump that hadn't shown up in her exam at the doctor's office.

Destinae didn't tell anyone at first, not even her husband. After a few days, the lump was still there, so she decided it needed to be checked out. A biopsy confirmed that Destinae had invasive ductal carcinoma—at age 30.

As any woman would be, Destinae was completely crushed by the news. Thankfully, an out-pouring of support from friends and family lifted Destinae back up. She also received support from a complete stranger—who would soon become a dear friend.

In February, Destinae received an unexpected package from a friend of a friend. Inside the package was a Lemongrass Spa Loving Gift Care Set and a note that said:

"I have no doubt you're scared, but you've got this! Don't hesitate to reach out to me anytime."

The amazing woman who sent Destinae this thoughtful gift and encouraging words is a registered nurse, Lemongrass Spa director, and mother of twin boys. She also sent Destinae a monetary donation from one of her fundraisers to help pay for Destinae's medications and co-pays.

All of the love and support buoyed Destinae. They helped her to get through the challenging time around her diagnosis.

"Most of my first month of diagnosis was a blur," Destinae said. "It didn't even seem like real life. I knew the information the doctors were telling me was serious and that my life was about to change drastically. I went into 'planner mode' and made my appointments and took lots of notes along the way while trying to stay emotionally stable for all of the people around me."

As hard as Destinae tried to protect her friends and her family—and herself—from the reality of the challenge she was facing, she couldn't do it indefinitely.

"When they placed my medication port, the reality of the diagnosis crashed down on me," Destinae remembered. "That's when I finally allowed myself the time to be scared and angry."

As Destinae started her treatments, she also began using the Lemongrass Spa products. Her new friend offered tips on using the products and gave her advice on what types of side effects she might have on her skin.

Destinae was grateful for the advice, and she was even more thankful for the Lemongrass Spa products that helped save her skin through her treatments. She had learned from her doctor and also from her own research online which chemicals and types of skin care products to avoid that might worsen side effects. But Destinae didn't find it as easy to identify which products to use that might *help.*

"The Lemongrass Spa products were a blessing," Destinae said. "They outshined anything else I could find in stores and online."

She used Lemongrass Spa Ultra Hydrating Crème daily all over—even on her head when she lost her hair. Even though the chemotherapy was affecting her skin, it never felt dry or damaged thanks to this product. Destinae found that the Organic Skin and Nail Balm was great for her nails and cuticles during treatment, and she continues to use it even today. Another one of her favorite products is the Healing Elements Balm.

"Healing Elements helped my scars heal after surgery," Destinae said. "It was my go-to cream to heal any skin irritations I experienced."

After Destinae completed her treatments, her life returned to normal. With her energy and free time increasing, she decided to join Lemongrass Spa as a consultant and wellness advocate.

"Now, I'm cancer free, and I'm thankful for the opportunity to share my love for Lemongrass Spa products," Destinae said. "I'm grateful to be able to share what I have learned with other people and to help them every day."

Gifting for Good

Working to raise money to fight cancer was a passionate cause for Madeline Gerris of Westfield, New Jersey, even before she had cancer. For 15 years before she was diagnosed with breast cancer at the age of 48, Madeline organized an annual breast cancer fundraiser in northern New Jersey. Between 150 and 200 ladies attended each year, eager to donate to the cause and educate themselves about the disease. Some of the speakers they had at the fundraisers were medical professionals, and survivors also educated the group about topics such as the importance of early detection and keeping a positive attitude. Madeline credits these fundraisers and their emphasis on the importance of self-breast exams for making her realize it had been awhile since she had done one. So she did her self-exam.

She found a lump.

Like many women, Madeline had fibrocystic breasts, which makes it more difficult to appreciate tumors during a self-exam. When Madeline went in for her mammogram, the radiologist didn't find anything at first. This is where Madeline stresses how important it is to be your own advocate.

"I insisted the radiologist look again and actually showed him where the lump was located," Madeline said.

Madeline's physician concluded that she did have breast cancer. In fact the mass was too large to have a partial mastectomy.

Because Madeline had a history of breast cancer in her family and because she had fibrocystic breast tissue, she opted for a double mastectomy to eliminate any chance of breast cancer reoccurrence in the future.

Madeline was cured of cancer with surgery, and she didn't require any chemotherapy or radiation treatments based on oncotype DX testing, which predicts the likelihood of cancer reoccurrence in a 10-year period. She also didn't lose too many lymph nodes thanks to the results of a sentinel node biopsy. Doctors are able to locate the lymph node associated with the tumor and test it for cancer. If it is negative for cancer, then it hasn't spread to other lymph nodes. This saves patients from potential problems like lymphedema.

Madeline tested negative for BRCA1 and BRCA2. The BRCA gene test is a blood test using DNA analysis to identify mutations in either one of the breast cancer susceptibility genes, called BRCA1 and BRCA2. Because the BRCA gene test can also be an indicator for ovarian cancer, a negative result for both these genes was a relief for Madeline.

"I was so relieved that I wouldn't need to have a hysterectomy to eliminate a genetic chance of ovarian cancer," Madeline said.

Soon after, Madeline's journey with breast cancer took her on a new path-one of giving back. Instead of having her cancer treated at a local hospital, she decided to go to Sloan Kettering Cancer Center in New York. She strongly advises that all cancer patients be treated

> "Each person holds so much power within themselves that needs to be let out. Sometimes they just need a little nudge, a little direction, a little support, a little coaching, and the greatest things can happen."
>
> —PETE CARROLL

at a medical facility that specializes in cancer, where all the new treatments are being developed and implemented.

While Madeline was being treated at the center, she decided to use her fashion business as a stylist with a jewelry company, Stella & Dot, to gift bracelets to breast cancer patients. Every year Stella & Dot designs a bracelet just for this purpose, and they donate a portion of the proceeds to organizations working to develop breast cancer awareness and cures. Madeline started looking for sponsors to buy the bracelets, and then she would place them in gift bags to give out to patients. It was a win/win for everybody.

But Madeleine came upon an obstacle. Sloan Kettering didn't allow companies or people to give gifts to patients. Madeline was quick to solve this problem, suggesting that she would remain anonymous. She delivered the bracelets for the staff to give out. The doctors and nurses enjoyed brightening their patients' days with the bracelets in their beautiful little gift bags. Giving them out became so popular, everyone needed to take turns. During one of Madeline's oncologist appointments, a nurse gave her a gift bag, and she discreetly disclosed that she was the anonymous person giving them out.

Madeline gifts around 50 bracelets every year. She enjoys every minute of giving back to the breast cancer community.

Along with fundraising and anonymous gift giving, Madeline also spends time offering one-on-one support to people in her community with cancer. Having walked through her own cancer journey, Madeline can offer emotional support and even clarify most of the medical procedures and jargon.

During Madeline's treatment, she had a terrific support system. She had friends to travel to New York with her for her appointments at Sloan Kettering. They would often grab lunch and spend the day in the city afterward. She also had her family, including her two boys Thomas, 20 and Jack, 16. She knows how important a support system is for patients battling cancer, and giving back by being there for others is important to her.

Madeline was diagnosed with cancer two years ago. In many ways, her life did not change. She was already active in cancer awareness, especially breast cancer. She did say her diagnosis helped her make the decision to get genetic testing done such as the BRCA1 and BRCA2 tests. It also helped her find new ways to give back, including gift giving to cancer patients and helping others going through cancer in her community.

Today, Madeline is now even busier than she was before cancer, holding down two jobs, one as a stylist with Stella & Dot and one as a personal shopper with Lord & Taylor. Everything she does reflects a positive attitude that's infectious to people around her. She helps so many with her gifts of understanding and compassion.

Thriving–not Just Surviving

As a single mother to three children, Carrie Madrid, 46, was busy working as a clinical conference coordinator to make ends meet. Until Carrie was diagnosed with cancer at age 41, she felt like she was in survival mode.

In addition to all the responsibilities of a single mom, Carrie was also active in her children's recreational activities. She was the booster president of the high school girls' basketball team, which involved fundraising for and supporting the group.

In November 2011, Carrie noticed two lumps in her breast. So began her journey with stage 3 infiltrating ductal carcinoma, which is also known as invasive ductal carcinoma.

Ironically, when Carrie's real life-saving battle began is when she switched into "serenity mode."

"When I found out that I had breast cancer, I didn't become hysterical or depressed," Carrie said. "Oddly, I felt peaceful. I was determined to win this battle."

Cancer became just one more obstacle in Carrie's life to overcome. Her survival instinct kicked in, and she was ready to fight.

At the same time, Carrie felt that her diagnosis was an opportunity to teach other people how to deal with a life-threatening illness. She wanted to be a role model for others on how to cope.

Carrie believed that her first opportunity to be a positive role model was for her children and the girls' basketball team she mentored. The coach told the team of Carrie's diagnosis.

Carrie was like a second mother to these young women, who call her Mama Carrie. Some of the girls were scared and cried when they heard that she had cancer. Most felt that she would survive.

Throughout Carrie's diagnosis and treatment, she wanted to show her daughters and the girls on her basketball team that she'd deal with this through "laughter and lip gloss." Carrie said that wearing lip gloss always makes her feel better. These became her words to live by.

Carrie's mastectomy was scheduled during their season finals. The girls made history and went to the California State Championship game the night after Carrie's first chemo treatment. That was the only game she wasn't able to attend. She cheered her girls on, watching them on TV.

As Carrie's long battle with cancer continued, she found herself looking at life differently. She looked at herself as a survivor, but she also felt that she was truly *living* for the first time in her life. Instead of just making it through her days, she began to live each moment mindfully.

Carrie reached out to her friends and family for help. "It really does take a village to battle cancer," Carrie said.

Carrie looked into finding a support group to add to her village, but nothing seemed to be the right fit for her.

Undaunted, Carrie decided to start her own organization. She gathered together other women suffering from breast cancer for group support and also to do activities together. Local businesses donated tickets and services for their outings. This got patients' minds off of cancer.

"I was thankful to have my family nearby to help me as I battled cancer," Carrie said.

Carrie noticed that other cancer patients didn't have access to the support they needed. They struggled to drive themselves to chemo treatments and to take care of their dependent family members. Being sick also puts a financial strain on patients and their dependents. Carrie realized there was a need in her town of Riverside, California, for emotional and financial support for many patients, male and female, struggling with breast cancer.

In 2014, Carrie's group was incorporated as the not-for-profit the CARE Project, Inc., to provide both emotional and financial support for families in need impacted by cancer. This remarkable organization offers gas cards to patients struggling to pay for trips to and from chemotherapy treatments. Grocery cards are also offered to help keep food on their tables.

Additionally, the CARE Project, Inc., offers a Pillar Grant, which is funded by the company Pillar CrossFit. Every year, a breast cancer patient in the community demonstrating financial need receives this grant. Children of patients are also given support around prom time for clothing and other expenses. These prom grants are $250 to $500 per student, and they help to take the financial burden of prom expenses off an ill parent.

Many of Carrie's volunteers in the CARE Project, Inc., come from the support group itself.

"I often have to tell people, 'Get better first! Then you can volunteer,'" Carrie said.

Most of their funding comes from an annual gala made possible by donations from the community. From the venue to the DJ, everyone helps out to support this important cause.

On January 31, 2017, the CARE Project, Inc., took up residence in its new office space. You can learn more about it at TheCareProjectInc.org.

Carrie still works hard to be a positive example and to better the lives of breast cancer survivors.

"I'm *living*, rather than just *surviving*, post cancer," Carrie said.

Carrie said she wouldn't change having breast cancer and all she has learned from the struggle. Her experience has positively impacted her life and also the lives of many others through her charity. She cherishes every day she shares with her children, son Anthony, 27, and daughters Mailisa, 20, and Olivia, 17.

Creating a New Good Place

Back in 2010, Stephanie Seban, now 37, was in a "good place." Stephanie was teaching English in Los Angeles, California, working on her master's degree, and dating a great guy.

"I finally felt like I was doing well," Stephanie remembered. "I felt like I was finally on the right path. Life was good."

When Stephanie found a lump in her breast, she didn't give it much thought. But over the next few months, practically before her eyes, the lump grew bigger and bigger.

"I knew that something was not right," Stephanie said.

She scheduled a mammogram appointment right away, and then she saw a gynecologist, who sent her for a biopsy. The nurse at the office told her she'd get the results in a week.

When the nurse called the next day, Stephanie knew it wasn't good news.

That's when her crazy journey began. Stephanie was diagnosed with stage 4 metastatic breast cancer. She was 31 years old.

"I don't have the BRCA genetic mutation. Nor did I have a family history of cancer," Stephanie said. "Cancer just happened to me. There's no medical explanation why."

Stephanie had a partial mastectomy. Because the surgeon feared she hadn't gotten all of the cancer, Stephanie needed to have two more surgeries. Because the surgeries and treatments are so time-consuming, Stephanie had to quit the teaching job she loved. Then she had to stop pursuing her master's degree. And then her promising relationship ended. Cancer had taken a great deal from Stephanie.

A few years later, a scan revealed that the cancer had spread to her lymph nodes, and then it had metastasized to her bones and lungs. The doctors told Stephanie that only 1 in 5 people with her type of cancer live for 5 years. She's going on 6.

Cancer took so much, but it couldn't take Stephanie's spirit.

"I'm very blessed to still be here," Stephanie said. "Every day is a gift. After being diagnosed with cancer, my focus changed. Now, I try to do something each day to appreciate life and creation."

Propelled by that spirit, Stephanie made sweeping changes in her life—to *live*.

"I had always been an over-achiever, hard-working almost to a fault," Stephanie said. "I eliminated a lot of stress from my life. I stopped putting so many expectations on myself. I used to be a 'yes' person, and I stopped saying 'yes' to everything. I also used to be a people pleaser, putting everyone else's happiness before my own. Now I put *me* first."

Considering the health challenges Stephanie faced, reducing stress wasn't going to be easy. To relax, Stephanie made more time to exercise—especially outside.

"When I'm outside, in nature, I feel closer to God," Stephanie said. "I started to spend a lot of time outdoors."

Stephanie brought her appreciation for nature inside as well. She stopped eating meat, started juicing, and began eating more organic foods. She also takes fistfuls of nutritional supplements, and she drinks alkaline water, which she said helps to make the body less acidic, discouraging the growth of cancer cells.

Trying out every possibility for good health, Stephanie has experimented with various alternative therapies, such as acupuncture, tapping, and meditation. She sees a Chinese herbalist, and she takes Chinese herbs.

"I feel that the herbs have been instrumental in keeping me healthy," Stephanie said. It's important to see an herbalist, however, and follow his or her recommendations.

The herbalist is just one of the many people on Stephanie's extensive anti-cancer team.

"My support team has played an enormous role in keeping me healthy and well," Stephanie said. "My mother has been key. She's been there for me the entire time. She goes with me to all of my appointments and treatments. My father has been so supportive as well. And I'm so blessed to have an amazing group of friends. I don't think I could have survived this without them."

Stephanie believes that friend and family support is critical to keeping a healthy mental state.

"Loving support is every bit as important as the cancer treatments are," Stephanie said.

Perhaps because Stephanie knows how helpful spirit and support have been to her, she was eager to create something to give back to other women facing similar cancer challenges. She launched a website, www.StephanieSeban.com, to help share what she had learned and to help other women. Stephanie's tagline offers a glimpse into what the site is all about: Believe. Live. Inspire.

"When I was diagnosed, I felt very alone and in the dark," Stephanie said. "A lot of women I met on my journey were a lot older than me. Many of them unfortunately passed away. When you're young and you have cancer, it creates a whole other set of circumstances, challenges, and issues. I'm such a researcher, and I had gathered so much information that I thought, *There must be other women out there like me. Why not share all of this with them?*"

So with the unwavering faith that "if you build it, they will come, Stephanie created her website.

She built it.

And they *did* come!

Stephanie has a large following and has created a community of young people fighting—and surviving--cancer. She answers their emails and questions, offering support and comfort.

"My hope is to keep growing my audience," Stephanie said. "I also want to help educate people that breast cancer is no longer a disease that affects the elderly. It's not your grandmother's disease, your great aunt's disease. It can affect your mother. Your sister. Your friend. You."

One of Stephanie's goals with her site is to help people understand that cancer isn't a death sentence. Just looking at photos of Stephanie herself on the site conveys this; she's youthful, vibrant, healthy, happy. Stephanie is literally the face of survival. In her blog and articles, she shows by example how she's living her life just like anyone else. There are many, many women thriving with stage 4 metastatic cancer. Stephanie offers hope and a community that understands.

"I have found my purpose in life," Stephanie said. "I want to inform and inspire people. I love that I'm still teaching—just in a new way."

Stephanie has created her own new good place.

Making Connections

No one should have to fight a challenge alone. Especially no one battling cancer.

Yet sadly, many warriors do.

When Noreen Culver, now 54, was diagnosed with cancer in 2010, she was made aware of just how many people are out there facing cancer alone. Noreen found that not everyone going through this difficult fight has friends and family to support them emotionally and physically. Many patients lack family members close by and need help getting to chemotherapy appointments. Some people need a friendly ear to listen to what they are going through.

So Noreen decided to make a difference.

She started to network, connecting patients with people offering support and counseling to anyone in her community who needs it. Mostly through word of mouth, she finds many people to help.

Noreen's own cancer story itself offers a powerful message. Noreen has the very common condition of fibrocystic breast tissue.

This simply means that her breasts have denser breast tissue and many benign lumps and bumps.

This condition itself does not cause any problems, but it can make finding malignant tumors a problem. That's what happened to Noreen.

Prior to her diagnosis in 2010 Noreen had felt a large lump that didn't feel right to her. Every year her mammograms came back normal, so Noreen's doctors told her not to worry about it. However, after her mammogram in 2010, the lump was getting larger and more painful.

Concerned, Noreen made an appointment to see her doctor. After he physically evaluated the lump, she was immediately sent for more diagnostic testing confirming she had breast cancer. That's when Noreen learned that her fibrocystic breast tissue delayed her malignancy diagnosis for many years.

It usually takes a few weeks to schedule surgery, but due to the gravity of Noreen's diagnosis, she was having surgery within a week. The surgeon performed a double mastectomy. Although the lump was in one breast, the tumor was endocrine receptor positive (estrogen or progesterone receptors), which means these two hormones were contributing to the growth of her cancer. Removing both breasts would eliminate the chance of cancer retuning to the same breast or the other one. Her treatment consisted of chemotherapy, reconstructive surgery, and radiation.

Noreen's journey with breast cancer brings up the concern of detection of breast cancer in women with the common condition of fibrocystic breasts.

"Women with fibrous breasts need to be their own advocates," Noreen said.

Years before her lump became painful, she felt something was wrong. In retrospect, she would have asked her doctor to examine the lump when she first felt it.

"Nobody knows your body better than you do," Noreen said. "Don't be afraid to speak up for it when your gut tells you something is wrong."

Another option for women with fibrocystic breasts is to go to breast centers that use digital mammography. These types of mammograms allow radiologists to change the contrast of light and dark on the computer. This gives them the ability to enlarge an area of breast tissue on the screen to closely examine areas of concern.

Also, consider having an ultrasound. Used in conjunction with digital mammography, a breast ultrasound is useful in differentiating normal findings from abnormal findings. It's important to keep in mind one does not replace the other. The digital mammogram is always the best starting point.

Noreen has important messages for people fighting cancer—and really for all of us.

"Because life is short and ever changing, do the things you've always wanted to do," Noreen said. She lives in rural Campbellsburg, Kentucky, and after her cancer diagnosis, she decided to take up hunting with her husband. She was always busy working two jobs, retail sales manager of several stores and leather crafter, and she never had time for this interest. Plus, she said growing up, this activity wasn't offered to her, only to the boys. So she started hunting and is now the owner of many different rifles.

"I hope to get a Thanksgiving turkey this year," Noreen said.

Noreen also left her management job go to focus on her true

> "*Optimism is the foundation of courage.*"
>
> —NICHOLAS MURRAY BUTLER

passion: leather crafting. She works on repairing leather products for equestrians and crafting original leather goods, such as custom belts. She has even made a pair of custom halters for two lucky cows.

"Being a leather crafter is my true passion," Noreen said. "Life is too short to be in an unhappy job."

Slowing down and letting other people help out is also another one of the important philosophies Noreen has learned from her journey with cancer. As a wife and mother of two, Michelle, 24, and Michael, 25, Noreen knows how busy life can get with family responsibilities.

She has also been an equestrian for the majority of her life, taking care of and training her own horses for years. Like anybody seriously committed to a sport, it's extremely difficult for horse people to sit back and let another person help out with their barn duties. After Noreen got home from one of her breast reconstructive surgeries, her daughter caught her trying to sneak out to the barn to take care of the horses. Michelle reminded her that the surgeon didn't want her in the barn due to the risk of infection, but letting go of her beloved barn duties was heartbreaking. Learning to let others take care of her was a process and not something that happened overnight. Cancer takes so much from people so quickly that it's only natural that adjusting to a new life will take time and effort.

Noreen has been enjoying a cancer free life for years now. Even with Noreen's late diagnosis due to her fibrocystic breasts, it did not change the 97 percent survival rate given for her type of cancer. Because treatments are becoming so effective, Noreen says there is hope for even later stage cancers.

Today, Noreen loves working at her own business, NC Tack Repairs, and she's moved from a storefront to working from home. This gives her more time to spend with her family, friends, and of course, her beloved dogs and horses. She is enjoying her new equine adventure driving miniature horses. Even seven years after her diagnosis, Noreen's still active in her community, offering guidance and help for people living with cancer.

Providing Pick-Me-Ups

Robin Leist believes we come into this world with a purpose. We may not know what it is, however, until we get a wake-up call.

For the past few years, Robin's daughter Tracy had been in charge of her purpose.

In 2012, after a fierce battle, Tracy died of breast cancer. She left her husband; three children; parents; brothers; her beloved sister-in-law, Heidi Leist; and a multitude of friends behind to face this world without her.

"The battle Tracy fought stays with us all," Robin said. "I was devastated. Having spent much of her last six months with her as I commuted between Colorado and Minnesota, I had come to know her in a special and life-changing way. She and I talked at great depth, sharing everything, holding back nothing."

Tracy's family remembers her as wise and witty.

"She gave her very best to all the people who came to visit her," Robin said. "They always went away with gifts of grace and wisdom from her."

Tracy had a career in marketing with Deluxe Corporation. Her mark is still on the home office, with her soaring spirit and sense of fun always present.

"I hear from Tracy's Deluxe friends all of the time," Robin said.

When Tracy lost her hair to chemotherapy, she became doubly determined to look her best anytime she was in public. She was not vain, but she believed that if she knew she looked great, she would feel better as well. She even tattooed her eyelids so that she could get out of bed looking smart and alert!

Tracy watched Lemongrass Spa Products grow from infancy to a major force. As a marketing expert, she gave Heidi and Bryan some ideas. She faithfully used Lemongrass Spa products to help her skin and scalp as she faced the effects of countless drugs.

"A few months after Tracy left us, I was driven to start Ittybags, Inc. to pass on her wisdom, her gentle, loving concern for her friends and family, her drive to move mountains, and to make the world a better place," Robin said. "Our products—Itty Games and Ittybags—bring fun and hope to people who need a pick-me-up. They light the way to personal growth and positivity, as Tracy herself did."

"Because Tracy showed such strength and positivity through her life's journey, my purpose, over the past few years, has been to continue her work, hoping to inspire folks to better, healthier, more positive life styles," Robin said.

Fighting Back with Style and Grace

"I felt incredulous."

That's how Lois Hazel remembers feeling when she found out she had stage 2B breast cancer.

"I was in the best shape of my life," Lois says. "I was only 54 years old and vibrantly healthy. I went to the gym three times a week, ate well, and had a good marriage and a deep spiritual life. Everything in my life was positive."

Lois's cancer diagnosis came at her out of far, far left field. There was absolutely no cancer history in her family.

"I was the trailblazer," Lois said ruefully.

Little did Lois know at the time, it was a rocky trail she was about to traverse.

Lois's physician found a 2.5-centimeter tumor in her breast. She underwent four biopsies to determine the cancer's stage. Then she had a procedure called a needle localization, which helps the surgeon to know exactly what tissue to remove to eliminate the tumor.

Lois underwent a mastectomy. At her checkup, she was excited to hear that her lymph nodes were clear. But that relief made it even harder to hear a few weeks later at her follow-up when final pathology revealed that the lymph nodes *weren't* all clear. Lois needed to have another surgery to remove the diseased lymph nodes.

"It's funny the things that bring you comfort, and the things that you remember," Lois said. "To this day, I remember that the nurse had the softest, gentlest hands. I'll always remember her kindness."

With the second surgery completed, Lois underwent four rounds of chemo, with a drug known to cause intense side effects. Yet she overcame each and every one with courage and style.

"My toenails fell off," Lois said. "My fingernails hurt so badly that it felt like they had been slammed in a car door. And they turned blue!"

So she covered them up with nail polish.

"My hair fell out," Lois said.

So she wore beautiful wigs and hats.

"My scalp itched like crazy!" Lois said.

So she dabbed on soothing witch hazel.

"My skin got dry and as parched as the Sahara desert," Lois said.

She found help and healing from all-natural skin products, such as those with shea butter. And she was careful to avoid parabans, which can spur the growth of cancer cells.

"I developed terrible nosebleeds," Lois said.

So she went to a specialist, who suggested she run a humidifier and put plugs of soft cotton covered with Vaseline in each nostril at night—one nostril at time so she could breathe.

"I had a lot of nausea, vomiting, and mouth sores," Lois said.

So she enjoyed as many popsicles as she could to ease the discomfort and pain. Yogurt also sometimes soothed her mouth

Finding a Way to Give Back

pain. She chose her foods carefully to avoid pain as much as she could.

Lois combatted every single challenge cancer threw at her with bravery and her sunny personality and cheer.

"If I hadn't been in such good shape emotionally, physically, and spiritually, I don't think I would have come through it all as well as I did," she said.

"Some days, I felt well," she remembered. "Other days, if I felt nauseated, I'd relax on the couch or in bed, knowing I'd feel better by the next day."

Along with Lois every step of the way on her journey were her supportive husband, Dale, and their two daughters, who were 29 and 28 years old at the time.

When Lois was five years cancer free, her family had a big celebration and trip to New York City.

"Five years without a recurrence is a big milestone," Lois said. "It's a very positive sign."

Today, Lois enjoys her wonderfully busy, active life, filled with her family and friends.

"I'm bought a kayak this summer," Lois says. "And I'm going back to cycling, which I enjoyed before I got sick. Bicycling makes me feel so good. I love to feel the breeze in my hair and on my face as I'm tooling along."

But most of all, what does Lois credit for her making it through so much, so well?

"I have a strong faith," Lois says. "I always firmly believe that God is going to take care of me. And He did."

About the Author and Photographer

Heidi and her sister, Kim, and brother, John, grew up in a small agricultural community near Milbank, South Dakota. Her parents, Millard and Karen Voeltz, owned and operated Western Lumber & Steel.

After graduating from high school with honors, Heidi attended the University of South Dakota in Vermillion and graduated with a B.S. in Business Administration with an Economics emphasis. She relocated to Denver, Colorado, and worked as the office administrator and treatment coordinator for a large dental practice in Littleton.

Heidi met her husband, Bryan, in Colorado, and they were married a year later. They have two remarkable daughters, Emily and Clara, who continue to be Heidi's inspiration for creating products without toxic chemicals.

Heidi started Lemongrass Spa Products after taking botanical blending courses and doing extensive research on natural ingredients. She began formulating bath and body care products and sourcing soap and lotion with local artisans while Emily was an infant and during her pregnancy with Clara.

Bryan Leist grew up in Las Cruces, New Mexico, with his parents, Jim and June. Prior to meeting Heidi, Bryan traveled extensively, providing English instruction in Moscow and Russia and delivering humanitarian aid in Croatia and Bosnia during the war in the former Yugoslavia. Bryan excelled as an IT Administrator and Software Support Manager.

In January of 2005, Bryan quit his job in the IT world to focus solely on promoting the future of Lemongrass Spa Products by concentrating on the daily operations and financial components of the business. Since then the Leists, along with their hardworking staff, have been committed to making this company what it is today.

Heidi is an active member of the Direct Selling Association where she has been a featured speaker at their Boot Camp for new members. She is a member of the Direct Selling Women's Association and Natural Ingredients Resource Center. She enjoys sharing the message of better health with a faith-based focus.

Bryan is an avid reader, boating enthusiast, and professional photographer. He and Heidi enjoy traveling, fishing, beachcombing, and working out with their teenage daughters.

Emily and Clara Leist at the 2017 Lemongrass Spa Products Convention

About the Author and Photographer

About Lemongrass Spa

Just like you, we wanted the best for our family but we couldn't find it...

When Lemongrass Spa Founder, Heidi, was pregnant with her daughter, she began reading labels on her skincare, makeup, and bath products and realized there were many toxins in everything she was using. On a mission to find safer products, she started creating her own bath crystals and tub teas. She and a friend hosted a girls' night out and showed women how to make their own natural bath crystals. It was that fun-filled evening that inspired Heidi to create more products and eventually provide spa experiences for women across the county.

From our home to a team of thousands!

Since their humble beginnings, Heidi and her mother, Karen, and a small staff of part-time moms worked together to create products in Heidi's home when the company first got started in the small mountain town of Bailey, Colorado. Soon thereafter, Heidi's husband, Bryan, quit his IT job to oversee software, accounting, and commissions. In 2007, Lemongrass Spa moved out of the Leist's home to a manufacturing and distribution center in Pine, Colorado, where some manufacturing and customer service still operate. In August 2014, a second manufacturing and distribution center opened in Tarpon Springs, Florida.

Founded on a belief that skincare and body care could be clean, simple, and natural, Lemongrass Spa has continued that tradition for 15 years. Priding themselves on creating 97 to 100 percent all-natural products, Heidi and Bryan go so far as to ensure that Lemongrass Spa Products are gluten-free, and many of them vegan. Focused on essential oils and botanical scenting, even the most discerning customers find their products to be soothing and exceptionally healing.

Lemongrass Spa Products was named to the 2014, 2015, and 2016 Top 100 Women Owned Companies in Colorado and Top 500 Companies in Manufacturing in the state. The company is endorsed by Beauty Without Bunnies (cruelty-free products) organization.

Creating a community of health-conscious consultants who share our values is the foundation of the Lemongrass Spa logo.

It's our desire to provide customers with superior ingredients, hosts with magical party experiences, and consultants with an easy business model with which to build a sustainable income.

Sales consultants enjoyed earning their trip to Jamaica in June of 2017.

Afterword: Making Lifestyle Changes

When you or a family member have been diagnosed with cancer, it's common to begin assessing everything you eat and drink. But what about what you put on your skin?

Ever since several studies[1] came out that linked parabens to breast cancer, people started taking notice of the toxic ingredients hidden in their lotions, shampoos, deodorants, and cosmetics. The majority of what you put on your skin is absorbed—up to 60 percent, according to experts—and can reach the blood stream. If you don't believe that, how do you explain how the nicotine patch works?

Studies prove that many chemicals found in products applied to the skin can actually reach your internal organs. They may accumulate in your tissues and become disruptive to your natural hormone balance. The concentration of these toxins over time can be dangerous—even life-threatening.

Finding natural and organic cosmetics, body wash, shampoo, and deodorants is fairly easy today. They're available online, at natural food stores, and Target. But finding brands you can trust that are committed to full disclosure and not just greenwashing is another story.

In developing the product line for Lemongrass Spa Products, it became very apparent to me that many major brands were using very few natural and organic ingredients, yet their labels implied the entire bottle of lotion was 100 percent plant based.

I encourage everyone to avoid the following ingredients to lower their exposure to toxins linked to disease.

First, avoid anything with parabens and phthalates in them. Any labels that includes "ethyl," "butyl," "methyl," and "propyl" are from the paraben family even if the word "paraben" isn't in the name. The American Chemical Society estimates that parabens are in about 85 percent of personal care products, ranging from shampoo to shaving cream. Researchers believe most of us get our greatest exposure from these products as they're absorbed through the skin. Phthalates, which are plasticizers, are much more difficult to determine. Products with fragrances that don't specifically state that they are phthalate-free probably do contain diethyl phthalate. It's linked to hormone disruption in people and bioaccumulation in the ocean, which becomes toxic to fish.

Second, I suggest you also avoid diethanolamine (DEA) and triethanolamine (TEA). These amines can react with nitrites to form nitrosamines, which have been strongly linked to cancer. Prevalent in a lot of skincare and cosmetics brands, these toxins are also harmful to fish and other wildlife when ingested or absorbed through skin.

Formaldehyde is another ingredient that's only allowed in very low concentrations because it's a probable carcinogen and skin irritant. I see it from time to time in nail polish, hair color, and eyelash adhesives. Ask your salon technician to check the label before you allow her to apply products.

Sunscreen has become one of the most sought after skincare products on the market, and unfortunately, it's one of the most toxic. Oxybenzone, an active ingredient in some chemical sunscreens, has been linked to cancer claims and a myriad of skin irritations. Just as disturbing is what it's doing to kill the ocean's coral reefs, particularly young coral. Octinoxate (Octylmethoxycinnamate) is also rated 'high' on the Environmental Working Group's Skin Deep Database Safe Sunscreen Guide. It can be a hormone disruptor and can be a skin allergen.

Spray-on sunscreens can be the most hazardous because butane is used as a propellant and can be absorbed by your skin. In some studies[2], applying spray-on sunscreens actually intensified the sun's rays instead of deflecting them!

Using a physical barrier sunscreen with zinc oxide and titanium dioxide is much safer. They are effective when applied often and preferable among homeopathic pundits.

If you're reaching for baby powder, think again. Talc, which happens to be the softest mineral available, is used in powder makeup and body powders to absorb wetness. Even though studies have proven inconclusive, there have been links to respiratory issues and ovarian cancer, which is why I tell everyone to avoid it. It's all about reducing risk! Look for powders containing arrowroot powder instead.

How many times a day do you think you wash your hands? When you're on the go, it's tempting to reach for hand sanitizer instead. The problem is that triclosan, an antimicrobial that acts as a preservative, is probably hidden inside the bottle. It's allowed in concentrations of up to 0.3 percent—even though it's been linked to cancer and endocrine disruption. Experts believe there's a possibility that triclosan can create antibiotic resistance in bacteria, not to mention toxicity to fish and other marine life. Using a low concentration of diluted essential oils that contains an antibacterial such as tea tree or lavender, is a good alternative.

The last ingredient I'll mention doesn't have a direct link to cancer, but because it's can be irritating to skin, you ought to be mindful of it. Sodium lauryl/laureth sulfate (SLS, SLES) is used to make soap foam up and suds. It can cause itchiness and dryness to the skin, especially when found in shampoos and lotions. SLS also has protein denaturing properties, which can cause epidermal damage.

Being an informed consumer is important, especially as a cancer survivor. Avoiding unnecessary toxins in food and drinks and also in skincare isn't difficult to do when you're armed with the information to make wise choices.

---

1 Leitman, Vulpe and their colleagues at the Silent Spring Institute published their findings online Oct. 27 in the journal Environmental Health Perspectives. The California Breast Cancer Research Program helped fund this research. Shawn Pan, Chaoshen Yuan, Abderrahmane Tagmount, Ruthann A. Rudel, Janet M. Ackerman, Paul Yaswen, Chris D. Vulpe, and Dale C. Leitman. 2015. Parabens and Human Epidermal Growth Factor Receptor Ligands Cross-Talk in Breast Cancer Cells. Environmental Health Perspectives.

2 Environmental Working Group, SkinDeep database. EWG has reviewed the existing data about human exposure and toxicity for the nine most commonly used sunscreen chemicals. The most worrisome is oxybenzone, added to nearly 65 percent of the non-mineral sunscreens in EWG's 2017 sunscreen database. Oxybenzone can cause allergic skin reactions (Rodriguez 2006). In laboratory studies it is a weak estrogen and has potent anti-androgenic effects (Krause 2012)